Financial Analysis with Texas Instruments Microcomputers

CHILTON'S COMPUTING SERIES

Financial Analysis with Texas Instruments Microcomputers

For the TI 99/4A and the TI Professional Computer

Joseph and Susan Berk

CHILTON BOOK COMPANY
Radnor, Pennsylvania

Copyright © 1984 by Joseph H. and Susan H. Berk
All Rights Reserved
Published in Radnor, Pennsylvania 19089 by Chilton Book Company
Designed by Arlene Putterman
Manufactured in the United States of America

Library of Congress Cataloging in Publication Data
Berk, Joseph H., 1951-
   Financial analysis with Texas Instruments microcomputers.
   (Chilton's computing series)
   Includes index.
   1. Business enterprises—Finance—Data processing.
2. Finance—Data processing. 3. Business mathematics—
Data processing. 4. TI 99/4A (Computer)—Programming.
5. Texas Instruments Professional Computer—Programming.
I. Berk, Susan H., 1955-   II. Title.
III. Series.
HG4012.5.B48   1984   658.1'5'02854   84-45158
ISBN 0-8019-7518-2 (pbk.)

Chilton's Computing Series

1 2 3 4 5 6 7 8 9 0   3 2 1 0 9 8 7 6 5 4

Contents

PREFACE ix

1 FINANCIAL RATIO ANALYSIS 1

Liquidity, Asset and Debt Management, and Profitability Ratios, 1
Sample Analysis: Assessing Past Performance, 2
Formulas, 7
Program Listing, 10

2 PERCENT INCOME STATEMENT ANALYSIS 15

Sample Analysis: Pinpointing Eroding Profitability, 15
Formula, 18
Program Listing, 19

3 COST-VOLUME-PROFIT ANALYSIS 21

Sample Analysis: Forecasting Net Income, 21
Formula, 23
Program Listing, 23

4 PRO FORMA FINANCIAL FORECASTING ANALYSIS   25

> The Four-Step Procedure, 25
> Sample Analysis: Costs of Supporting Sales Increase, 26
> Formulas, 31
> Program Listing, 32

5 COST OF CAPITAL ANALYSIS   35

> Five Cost Categories for Examination, 35
> Sample Analysis: Developing New Product, 37
> Formulas, 44
> Program Listing, 45

6 DEPRECIATION ANALYSIS   50

> Normal Depreciation, 50
> Accelerated Depreciation, 51
> Sample Analysis: Determining Best Depreciation Method, 52
> Formulas, 57
> Program Listing, 58

7 CORRELATION AND REGRESSION ANALYSIS   62

> Establishing Correlation Coefficients, 62
> Using Regression to Predict Dependent Variables, 63
> Sample Analysis: Commissions vs. Sales Volume, 64
> Sample Analysis: How Price Affects Volume, 70
> Sample Analysis: Ad Budget vs. Sales Volume, 73
> Formulas, 77
> Program Listing, 78

8 MULTIPLE LINEAR REGRESSION ANALYSIS   81

> Sample Analysis: Assessing the Effects of Several Variables on Sales Volume, 82
> Formulas, 85
> Program Listing, 86

9 INVENTORY LEVEL ANALYSIS   90

> Establishing EOQ and Safety Stock, 90
> Sample Analysis: Determining Optimal Inventory, 92
> Formulas, 95
> Program Listing, 98

10 PORTFOLIO ANALYSIS — 102

Understanding Beta Coefficients, 102
Sample Analysis: Reducing the Risk, 104
Formulas, 111
Program Listing, 112

11 DISCOUNT ANALYSIS — 114

Sample Analysis: Counting a Discount, 114
Formula, 115
Program Listing, 116

12 EFFECTIVE ANNUAL INTEREST RATE ANALYSIS — 117

Sample Analysis: Earning Interest on Interest, 117
Sample Analysis: Variable Interest and Compounding Rates, 121
Formulas, 122
Program Listing, 123

13 FUTURE VALUE ANALYSIS — 125

Sample Analysis: A 5-Year CD, 125
Sample Analysis: Pay Now/Pay Later?, 126
Formula, 127
Program Listing, 128

14 FUTURE VALUE OF AN ANNUITY ANALYSIS — 130

Sample Analysis: Payroll Savings, 130
Sample Analysis: Calculating Two Annuities, 133
Formulas, 136
Program Listing, 137

15 PRESENT VALUE ANALYSIS — 139

Sample Analysis: Investing Now for a Fixed Return, 139
Sample Analysis: Determining Smallest Present Value, 140
Formula, 143
Program Listing, 144

16 PRESENT VALUE OF AN ANNUITY ANALYSIS — 146

Sample Analysis: Exact Account Depletion, 146
Sample Analysis: Comparing Payment Methods, 148

Sample Analysis: Adjusting for Interest-Rate Changes, 149
Sample Analysis: Adjusting the Compounding Rates, 150
Formulas, 151
Program Listing, 152

17 PERPETUITY ANALYSIS — 155

Sample Analysis: An Immediate Perpetuity, 155
Sample Analysis: A Deferred Perpetuity, 157
Sample Analysis: Perpetuity vs. Cash Settlement, 158
Formulas, 159
Program Listing, 160

18 NET PRESENT VALUE ANALYSIS — 163

Sample Analysis: Three Oil-Exploration Projects, 164
Formulas, 167
Program Listing, 168

INDEX — 171

Preface

Texas Instruments microcomputers are among the best of the new generation of home computers. Although the TI-99/4A is inexpensive compared to some of the machines on the market, it has amazing capabilities. The new Texas Instruments Professional Computer has some of the most advanced features available at any price. Both are very powerful analytical tools.

This book makes good use of both machines' capabilities. The programs are written in powerful TI BASIC, and they can be used on the TI-99/4A computer exactly as they appear in this book. We've designed every program so that by changing only one statement, each will also run on the Texas Instruments Professional Computer. That's the CALL CLEAR statement, which clears the screen for the TI-99/4A. If you're using the Professional Computer, just replace the CALL CLEAR statement with PRINT CHR$(12).

The programs in this book will allow you to perform a variety of financial calculations. The information they provide can be used for stock or banking investment analysis. Crucial business decisions, such as profit prediction or project selection, can be made in a more informed manner. Even personal financial decisions will benefit from the use of these programs. Whether you are an investor, a business person, a student, or just interested in saving money with your Texas Instruments computer, this is the book for you: You'll learn a little about financial analysis, have some fun, and maybe even make money.

Financial Analysis with Texas Instruments Microcomputers

Financial Ratio Analysis
1

Financial ratio analysis is often used for assessing the performance and strength of a company. We'll examine four categories of ratios: liquidity, asset management, debt, and profitability.

LIQUIDITY, ASSET AND DEBT MANAGEMENT, AND PROFITABILITY RATIOS

LIQUIDITY RATIOS

Liquidity ratios provide an indication of a company's ability to meet its financial obligations. The current assets ratio is simply the ratio of current assets to current liabilities. The quick assets ratio is very similar, except that it does not include inventory. The quick assets ratio tells us if a company can quickly meet its obligations without having to sell inventory.

ASSET MANAGEMENT RATIOS

Asset management ratios measure how well a company uses its assets. The inventory turnover ratio tells how often the company sells its inventory in the accounting period. The average collection period tells how much time (in days) the company takes to collect accounts receivable. The fixed assets ratio is used to measure how well the company uses its plant and equipment. In a similar manner, the total assets ratio examines how well the company uses all of its assets.

DEBT MANAGEMENT RATIOS

Debt management ratios measure how much the company relies on borrowing, and how well it uses borrowed money. The debt ratio equals total debt divided by total assets. The times interest earned ratio shows by how many times earnings exceed interest payments.

PROFITABILITY RATIOS

The profitability ratios are probably the most important, because they show how well a company is doing on the bottom line. The profit margin on sales ratio reflects the company's net profit margin. Return on total assets is the ratio of net income to total assets (often referred to as ROA), and return on equity is the ratio of net income to the stockholders' investment (often referred to as ROE).

SAMPLE ANALYSIS: ASSESSING PAST PERFORMANCE

Tables 1.1 and 1.2 show balance sheets and income statements for the Acme Manufacturing Company for the last two years.

TABLE 1.1
Acme Manufacturing Company
Balance Sheets for Year Ending December 31

	1981	1982
ASSETS		
Cash	$150,000	$170,000
Accounts Receivable	300,000	330,000
Inventories	420,000	410,000
Total Current Assets	$870,000	$910,000
Property, Plant, and Equipment	$570,000	$570,000
Total Assets	$1,440,000	$1,480,000
LIABILITIES AND EQUITIES		
Accounts Payable	$120,000	$140,000
Notes Payable	80,000	75,000
Accrued Wages	10,000	11,000
Total Current Liabilities	$210,000	$226,000
First Mortgage Bonds	$300,000	$320,000
Debentures	100,000	60,000
Total Debt	$400,000	$380,000
Stockholders' Equity	$830,000	$874,000
Total Liabilities and Equities	$1,440,000	$1,480,000

Berk & Berk: *Financial Analysis with Texas Instruments Microcomputers* (Chilton)

TABLE 1.2
Acme Manufacturing Company
Income Statements for Year Ending December 31

	1981	1982
Sales	$950,000	$980,000
Expenses		
Commissions	100,000	120,000
Raw Materials	500,000	540,000
Maintenance	10,000	10,000
Earnings Before Interest and Taxes	$340,000	$310,000
Interest	$140,000	$120,000
Taxes	$100,000	$95,000
Net Income	$100,000	$95,000

Let's examine Acme's performance for the last two years and see how it's done; although we're only going to look at two years, the program can perform the analysis for any number of years. Load the Financial Ratio Analysis program into your TI-99/4A (the program listing begins on page 10), enter the command RUN, and here's what the computer will ask for:

Computer Request	Operator Input
WHAT IS THE NAME OF THE COMPANY?	ACME MANUFACTURING
HOW MANY PERIODS ARE BEING COMPARED?	2
WHAT IS THE FIRST PERIOD OF COMPARISON?	1981
WHAT ARE THE CURRENT ASSETS FOR 1981?	870000
WHAT ARE THE CURRENT LIABILITIES FOR 1981?	210000
WHAT IS THE INVENTORY FOR 1981?	420000
WHAT ARE THE SALES FOR 1981?	950000
WHAT ARE THE ACCOUNTS RECEIVABLE FOR 1981?	300000
WHAT ARE THE FIXED ASSETS FOR 1981?	570000

Berk & Berk: Financial Analysis with Texas Instruments Microcomputers (Chilton)

Computer Request	Operator Input
WHAT ARE THE TOTAL ASSETS FOR 1981?	1440000
WHAT IS THE TOTAL DEBT FOR 1981?	400000
WHAT IS THE EBIT FOR 1981?	340000
WHAT ARE THE INTEREST CHARGES FOR 1981?	140000
WHAT IS THE NPAT FOR 1981?	100000
WHAT IS THE COMMON EQUITY FOR 1981?	830000
WHAT ARE THE CURRENT ASSETS FOR 1982?	910000
WHAT ARE THE CURRENT LIABILITIES FOR 1982?	226000
WHAT IS THE INVENTORY FOR 1982?	410000
WHAT ARE THE SALES FOR 1982?	980000
WHAT ARE THE ACCOUNTS RECEIVABLE FOR 1982?	330000
WHAT ARE THE FIXED ASSETS FOR 1982?	570000
WHAT ARE THE TOTAL ASSETS FOR 1982?	1480000
WHAT IS THE TOTAL DEBT FOR 1982?	380000
WHAT IS THE EBIT FOR 1982?	310000

Computer Request	Operator Input
WHAT ARE THE INTEREST CHARGES FOR 1982?	120000
WHAT IS THE NPAT FOR 1982?	95000
WHAT IS THE COMMON EQUITY FOR 1982?	874000

At this point, the screen will clear and the computer will present the result of the financial ratio analysis:

```
FINANCIAL RATIO ANALYSIS FOR
ACME MANUFACTURING
PRESS ENTER TO CONTINUE
?
```

(press enter, the screen will clear, and you'll see . . .)

```
THE CURRENT ASSETS RATIOS
     1981   4.142857143
     1982   4.026548673
PRESS ENTER TO CONTINUE
?
```

(press enter, the screen will clear, and you'll see . . .)

```
THE QUICK RATIOS
     1981   2.142857143
     1982   2.212389381
PRESS ENTER TO CONTINUE
?
```

(press enter, the screen will clear, and you'll see . . .)

```
THE INVENTORY
TURNOVER RATIOS
     1981   2.261904762
     1982   2.390243902
PRESS ENTER TO CONTINUE
?
```

(press enter, the screen will clear, and you'll see . . .)

THE AVERAGE
COLLECTION PERIODS

    1981 115.2631579
    1982 122.9081633

PRESS ENTER TO CONTINUE
?

    (press enter, the screen will clear, and you'll see . . .)

THE FIXED ASSETS RATIOS

    1981 1.666666667
    1982 1.719298246

PRESS ENTER TO CONTINUE
?

    (press enter, the screen will clear, and you'll see . . .)

THE TOTAL ASSETS RATIOS

    1981 .6597222222
    1982 .6621621622

PRESS ENTER TO CONTINUE
?

    (press enter, the screen will clear, and you'll see . . .)

THE DEBT RATIOS

    1981 .2777777778
    1982 .2567567568

PRESS ENTER TO CONTINUE
?

    (press enter, the screen will clear, and you'll see . . .)

THE TIMES INTEREST
EARNED RATIOS

    1981 2.428571429
    1982 2.583333333

PRESS ENTER TO CONTINUE
?

    (press enter, the screen will clear, and you'll see . . .)

THE PROFIT MARGIN ON
SALES RATIO

    1981 .1052631579
    1982 .0969387755

```
PRESS ENTER TO CONTINUE
?
```
   (press enter, the screen will clear, and you'll see . . .)
```
THE RETURN ON ASSETS RATIOS
     1981  .0694444444
     1982  .0641891892
PRESS ENTER TO CONTINUE
?
```
   (press enter, the screen will clear, and you'll see . . .)
```
THE RETURN ON EQUITY RATIOS
     1981  .1204819277
     1982  .1086956522
** DONE **
```

  The ratio analysis tells us several things about Acme. The company has increased its ability to quickly raise cash to meet its debts, as shown by the improving *quick ratio*. Asset management is marginally better, as shown by the *fixed assets*, the *total assets*, and the *inventory turnover ratios*. The *debt ratio* shows debt has gone down slightly (compared to total assets), while the *times interest earned ratio* shows the company is earning more with respect to the amount of money it has borrowed. The first hint of a negative trend shows up in the *average collection period*. Here we see the company is taking longer to collect money owed. We can see the best indication of how the company is doing when we look at the profitability ratios. *Profit margin on sales, return on assets*, and *return on equity* are all down. Unless this trend is reversed, Acme will soon be in trouble. If you were considering buying stock in Acme, you should think again.

FORMULAS

All eleven formulas are included in the Program Listing; they are reviewed here for reference only.

CURRENT ASSETS RATIO

   $CR = CA/CL$ (see program line 800)

where

CR = current assets ratio
CA = current assets
CL = current liabilities

QUICK RATIO

$$QU = (CA - IN)/CL \quad \text{(see program line 810)}$$

where

QU = quick ratio
CA = current assets
IN = inventory value
CL = current liabilities

INVENTORY TURNOVER RATIO

$$T = SA/IN \quad \text{(see program line 820)}$$

where

T = turnover ratio
SA = sales
IN = inventory value

AVERAGE COLLECTION PERIODS

$$AC = AR*365/SA \quad \text{(see program line 830)}$$

where

AC = average collection period, in days
AR = accounts receivable
SA = sales

FIXED ASSETS RATIO

$$FR = SA/FA \quad \text{(see program line 840)}$$

where

FR = fixed assets ratio

SA = sales
FA = fixed assets

TOTAL ASSETS RATIO

$$TR = SA/TA \quad \text{(see program line 850)}$$

where

TR = total assets ratio
SA = sales
TA = total assets

DEBT RATIO

$$DR = TD/TA \quad \text{(see program line 860)}$$

where

DR = debt ratio
TD = total debt
TA = total assets

TIMES INTEREST EARNED RATIO

$$TI = EB/IT \quad \text{(see program line 870)}$$

where

TI = times interest earned ratio
EB = earnings before interest and taxes
IT = interest

PROFIT MARGIN ON SALES RATIO

$$PM = NP/SA \quad \text{(see program line 880)}$$

where

PM = profit margin on sales ratio
NP = net profit after taxes
SA = sales

RETURN ON ASSETS RATIO

$$RA = NP/TA \quad \text{(see program line 890)}$$

where

RA = return on assets ratio
NP = net profit after taxes
TA = total assets

RETURN ON EQUITY RATIO

$$RE = NP/CE \quad \text{(see program line 900)}$$

where

RE = return on equity ratio
NP = net profit after taxes
CE = common equity

PROGRAM LISTING

FINANCIAL RATIO ANALYSIS

```
100 CALL CLEAR
110 PRINT "WHAT IS THE NAME"
120 PRINT "OF THE COMPANY";
130 INPUT A$
140 PRINT
150 PRINT "HOW MANY PERIODS"
160 PRINT "ARE BEING COMPARED";
170 INPUT N
180 PRINT
190 PRINT "WHAT IS THE FIRST"
200 PRINT "PERIOD OF COMPARISON";
210 INPUT YE(1)
220 FOR I=1 TO N
230 YE(I)=YE(1)+I-1
240 PRINT
250 PRINT "WHAT ARE THE"
260 PRINT "CURRENT ASSETS"
270 PRINT "FOR";YE(I);
280 INPUT CA
```

Note: If using the TI Professional Computer, substitute PRINT CHR$(12) for CALL CLEAR.

```
290 PRINT
300 PRINT "WHAT ARE THE"
310 PRINT "CURRENT LIABILITIES"
320 PRINT "FOR";YE(I);
330 INPUT CL
340 PRINT
350 PRINT "WHAT IS THE"
360 PRINT "INVENTORY FOR";YE(I);
370 INPUT IN
380 PRINT
390 PRINT "WHAT ARE THE"
400 PRINT "SALES FOR";YE(I);
410 INPUT SA
420 PRINT
430 PRINT "WHAT ARE THE"
440 PRINT "ACCOUNTS RECEIVABLE"
450 PRINT "FOR";YE(I);
460 INPUT AR
470 PRINT
480 PRINT "WHAT ARE THE"
490 PRINT "FIXED ASSETS"
500 PRINT "FOR";YE(I);
510 INPUT FA
520 PRINT
530 PRINT "WHAT ARE THE"
540 PRINT "TOTAL ASSETS"
550 PRINT "FOR";YE(I);
560 INPUT TA
570 PRINT
580 PRINT "WHAT IS THE"
590 RPITN "TOTAL DEBT"
600 PRINT "FOR";YE(I);
610 INPUT TD
620 PRINT
630 PRINT "WHAT IS THE"
640 PRINT "EBIT FOR";YE(I);
650 INPUT EB
660 PRINT
670 PRINT "WHAT ARE THE"
680 PRINT "INTEREST CHARGES"
690 PRINT "FOR";YE(I);
700 INPUT IT
710 PRINT
720 PRINT "WHAT IS THE"
730 PRINT "NPAT FOR";YE(I);
740 INPUT NP
750 PRINT
```

```
760 PRINT "WHAT IS THE"
770 PRINT "COMMON EQUITY"
780 PRINT "FOR";YE(I);
790 INPUT CE
800 CR(I)=CA/CL
810 QU(I)=(CA-IN)/CL
820 T(I)=SA/IN
830 AC(I)=AR*365/SA
840 FR(I)=SA/FA
850 TR(I)=SA/TA
860 DR(I)=TD/TA
870 TI(I)=EB/IT
880 PM(I)=NP/SA
890 RA(I)=NP/TA
900 RE(I)=NP/CE
910 NEXT I
920 CALL CLEAR
930 PRINT "FINANCIAL RATIO ANALYSIS FOR"
940 PRINT A$
950 PRINT
960 PRINT
970 PRINT
980 PRINT
990 PRINT
1000 PRINT
1010 PRINT "PRESS ENTER TO CONTINUE"
1020 INPUT B$
1030 CALL CLEAR
1040 PRINT "THE CURRENT ASSETS RATIOS"
1050 PRINT
1060 PRINT
1070 FOR I=1 TO N
1080 PRINT YE(I);CR(I)
1090 NEXT I
1100 PRINT
1110 PRINT "PRESS ENTER TO CONTINUE"
1120 INPUT B$
1130 CALL CLEAR
1140 PRINT "THE QUICK RATIOS"
1150 PRINT
1160 PRINT
1170 FOR I=1 TO N
1180 PRINT YE(I);QU(I)
1190 NEXT I
1200 PRINT
1210 PRINT "PRESS ENTER TO CONTINUE"
1220 INPUT B$
```

```
1230 CALL CLEAR
1240 PRINT "THE INVENTORY"
1250 PRINT "TURNOVER RATIOS"
1260 PRINT
1270 PRINT
1280 FOR I = 1 TO N
1290 PRINT YE(I);T(I)
1300 NEXT I
1310 PRINT
1320 PRINT "PRESS ENTER TO CONTINUE"
1330 INPUT B$
1340 CALL CLEAR
1350 PRINT "THE AVERAGE"
1360 PRINT "COLLECTION PERIODS"
1370 PRINT
1380 PRINT
1390 FOR I = 1 TO N
1400 PRINT YE(I);AC(I)
1410 NEXT I
1420 PRINT
1430 PRINT "PRESS ENTER TO CONTINUE"
1440 INPUT B$
1450 CALL CLEAR
1460 PRINT "THE FIXED ASSETS RATIOS"
1470 PRINT
1480 PRINT
1490 FOR I = 1 TO N
1500 PRINT YE(I);FR(I)
1510 NEXT I
1520 PRINT
1530 PRINT "PRESS ENTER TO CONTINUE"
1540 INPUT B$
1550 CALL CLEAR
1560 PRINT "THE TOTAL ASSETS RATIOS"
1570 PRINT
1580 PRINT
1590 FOR I = 1 TO N
1600 PRINT YE(I);TR(I)
1610 NEXT I
1620 PRINT
1630 PRINT "PRESS ENTER TO CONTINUE"
1640 INPUT B$
1650 CALL CLEAR
1660 PRINT "THE DEBT RATIOS"
1670 PRINT
1680 PRINT
1690 FOR I = 1 TO N
```

```
1700 PRINT YE(I);DR(I)
1710 NEXT I
1720 PRINT
1730 PRINT "PRESS ENTER TO CONTINUE"
1740 INPUT B$
1750 CALL CLEAR
1760 PRINT "THE TIMES INTEREST"
1770 PRINT "EARNED RATIOS"
1780 PRINT
1790 PRINT
1800 FOR I=1 TO N
1810 PRINT YE(I);TI(I)
1820 NEXT I
1830 PRINT
1840 PRINT "PRESS ENTER TO CONTINUE"
1850 INPUT B$
1860 PRINT
1870 CALL CLEAR
1880 PRINT "THE PROFIT MARGIN ON"
1890 PRINT "SALES RATIOS"
1900 PRINT
1910 PRINT
1920 FOR I=1 TO N
1930 PRINT YE(I);PM(I)
1940 NEXT I
1950 PRINT
1960 PRINT "PRESS ENTER TO CONTINUE"
1970 INPUT B$
1980 CALL CLEAR
1990 PRINT "THE RETURN ON ASSETS RATIOS"
2000 PRINT
2010 PRINT
2020 FOR I=1 TO N
2030 PRINT YE(I);RA(I)
2040 NEXT I
2050 PRINT
2960 PRINT "PRESS ENTER TO CONTINUE"
2070 INPUT B$
2080 CALL CLEAR
2090 PRINT "THE RETURN ON EQUITY RATIOS"
2100 PRINT
2110 PRINT
2120 FOR I=1 TO N
2130 PRINT YE(I);RE(I)
2140 NEXT I
2150 END
```

Percent Income Statement Analysis

2

Percent income statement analysis is a specialized form of ratio analysis. This analysis converts all entries in the income statement to a percentage of sales for that year. If this is done for several years, trends can often be identified. Similarly, the analysis may be done for different companies to compare relative performance.

SAMPLE ANALYSIS: PINPOINTING ERODING PROFITABILITY

Table 2.1 shows a three-year income statement for the Newhall Sales Corporation.

TABLE 2.1
Newhall Sales Corporation
Income Statements for Year Ending December 31.

	1980	1981	1982
Sales	$102,000	$123,000	$154,000
Expenses			
Cost of Goods Sold	65,000	80,000	104,000
Sales Commissions	9,000	10,000	12,000
Taxes	5,000	9,000	13,000
Net Income	$23,000	$24,000	$25,000

Let's perform a percent income statement analysis for Newhall Sales Corporation. Load the program on page 19 into your TI-99/4A, enter the command RUN, and here's what the computer will ask for:

Computer Request	Operator Input
WHAT IS THE NAME OF THE COMPANY?	NEWHALL SALES CORPORATION
HOW MANY YEARS ARE BEING COMPARED?	3
WHAT IS THE FIRST YEAR OF COMPARISON?	1980
HOW MANY LINE ENTRIES ARE THERE ON THE INCOME STATEMENT?	5
WHAT IS THE DESCRIPTOR FOR EACH LINE?	
(ENTER SALES FIRST, THEN OTHERS, SUCH AS ADVERTISING, ETC.)	
?	SALES
?	COST OF GOODS SOLD
?	SALES COMMISSIONS
?	TAXES
?	NET INCOME
SALES FOR 1980?	102000
COST OF GOODS SOLD FOR 1980?	65000
SALES COMMISSIONS FOR 1980?	9000
TAXES FOR 1980?	5000
NET INCOME FOR 1980?	23000
SALES FOR 1981?	123000
COST OF GOODS SOLD FOR 1981?	80000
SALES COMMISSIONS FOR 1981?	10000

Computer Request	Operator Input
TAXES FOR 1981?	9000
NET INCOME FOR 1981?	24000
SALES FOR 1982?	154000
COST OF GOODS SOLD FOR 1982?	104000
SALES COMMISSIONS FOR 1982?	12000
TAXES FOR 1982?	13000
NET INCOME FOR 1982?	25000

Once you've entered the above information, the screen will clear, and here's what you'll see:

PERCENT INCOME STATEMENT
ANALYSIS FOR
NEWHALL SALES CORPORATION

PRESS ENTER TO CONTINUE
?

(press enter, the screen will clear, and you'll see . . .)

SALES
AS A PERCENT OF SALES
     1980 100
     1981 100
     1982 100

PRESS ENTER TO CONTINUE
?

(press enter, the screen will clear, and you'll see . . .)

COST OF GOODS SOLD
AS A PERCENT OF SALES
     1980 63.7254902
     1981 65.04065041
     1982 67.53246753

PRESS ENTER TO CONTINUE
?

(press enter, the screen will clear, and you'll see . . .)

SALES COMMISSIONS
AS A PERCENT OF SALES
    1980 8.823529412
    1981 8.130081301
    1982 7.792207792

PRESS ENTER TO CONTINUE
?

(press enter, the screen will clear, and you'll see . . .)

TAXES
AS A PERCENT OF SALES
    1980 4.901960784
    1981 7.317073171
    1982 8.441558442

PRESS ENTER TO CONTINUE
?

(press enter, the screen will clear, and you'll see . . .)

NET INCOME
AS A PERCENT OF SALES
    1980 22.54901961
    1981 19.51219512
    1982 16.23376623

** DONE **

We can see several interesting trends by examining the percent income statement analysis the TI just performed for us. First, the *cost of goods sold* has increased relative to sales for the last three years. This is an undesirable trend. The *sales commissions* have increased in absolute dollars (which should keep the sales people happy) but have decreased relative to sales (which should make the managers and stockholders of Newhall happy). Taxes have increased relative to sales, which suggests that the company is not doing as good a job as it could to minimize its tax liability. Finally, when we look at the bottom line, we see that net income (as a percent of sales) shows a downward trend. This is interesting, because even though net income increased for each year, we can readily see that Newhall's profitability is eroding.

FORMULA

The formula is included in the Program Listing; it is reviewed here for your reference only.

PERCENT OF SALES

$$PERCENT = AMT/SALES \quad \text{(see program line 460)}$$

where

PERCENT = the percent of sales
AMT = amount of each income statement line entry (i.e., advertising, taxes)
SALES = the sales

PROGRAM LISTING

PERCENT INCOME STATEMENT ANALYSIS

```
100 CALL CLEAR
110 DIM LI$(20),AMT(20,20),PERCENT(20,20)
120 PRINT "WHAT IS THE NAME"
130 PRINT "OF THE COMPANY";
140 INPUT NA$
150 PRINT
160 PRINT "HOW MANY YEARS ARE"
170 PRINT "BEING COMPARED";
180 INPUT N
190 PRINT
200 PRINT "WHAT IS THE FIRST"
210 PRINT "YEAR OF COMPARISON";
220 INPUT FIRST
230 PRINT
240 PRINT "HOW MANY LINE ENTRIES"
250 PRINT "ARE THERE ON"
260 PRINT "THE INCOME STATEMENT";
270 INPUT L
280 CALL CLEAR
290 PRINT
300 PRINT "WHAT IS THE DESCRIPTOR"
310 PRINT "FOR EACH LINE"
320 PRINT
330 PRINT "(ENTER SALES FIRST, THEN"
340 PRINT "OTHERS, SUCH AS"
350 PRINT "ADVERTISING, ETC.)"
360 FOR I=1 TO L
370 INPUT LI$(I)
380 NEXT I
390 CALL CLEAR
400 FOR J=1 TO N
```

Note: If using the TI Professional Computer, substitute PRINT CHR$(12) for CALL CLEAR.

```
410 FOR I=1 TO L
420 PRINT
430 PRINT LI$(I)
440 PRINT "FOR"; FIRST
450 INPUT AMT(I,J)
460 PERCENT (I,J)=100*AMT(I,J)/AMT(1,J)
470 NEXT I
480 CALL CLEAR
490 NEXT J
500 PRINT "PERCENT INCOME STATEMENT"
510 PRINT "ANALYSIS FOR"
520 PRINT NA$
530 PRINT
540 PRINT
550 PRINT
560 PRINT
570 PRINT
580 PRINT "PRESS ENTER TO CONTINUE"
590 INPUT B$
600 CALL CLEAR
610 FOR I=1 TO L
620 PRINT LI$(I)
630 PRINT "AS A PERCENT OF SALES"
640 PRINT
650 FOR J=1 TO N
660 PRINT FIRST+J−1;PERCENT(I,J)
670 NEXT J
680 PRINT
690 IF I=L THEN 740
700 PRINT "PRESS ENTER TO CONTINUE"
710 INPUT B$
720 CALL CLEAR
730 NEXT I
740 END
```

Cost-Volume-Profit Analysis
3

Cost-volume-profit analysis is used to determine how the fixed costs and variable costs affect the net income of a company. Variable costs are the costs directly associated with each unit of product manufactured. These costs are for expenses, such as the raw materials used, the commission paid, or the labor cost of each unit of product. Fixed costs, on the other hand, are independent of the number of units. General and administrative expenses, along with any other expenses not directly related to the number of units built, fall into this category.

SAMPLE ANALYSIS: FORECASTING NET INCOME

The Baker Manufacturing Company wishes to build 4000 units of Product 1, 2000 units of Product 2, 7000 units of Product 3, and 1500 units of Product 4. The company is taxed at the 50% level. The selling prices and variable costs of each product are shown in Table 3.1. The company's fixed costs total $11,000, and management would like to know what the net income will be.

Load the Cost-Volume-Profit Analysis program listed on page 23 into your TI-99/4A, enter the command RUN, and here's what the computer will ask for:

Computer Request	Operator Input
HOW MANY PRODUCTS ARE IN THE PRODUCT LINE?	4
HOW MANY UNITS OF PRODUCT 1 ARE THERE?	4000
HOW MANY UNITS OF PRODUCT 2 ARE THERE?	2000
HOW MANY UNITS OF PRODUCT 3 ARE THERE?	7000
HOW MANY UNITS OF PRODUCT 4 ARE THERE?	1500
WHAT IS THE TAX RATE?	.50
WHAT IS THE SALES PRICE OF PRODUCT 1?	1.25
WHAT IS THE VARIABLE COST OF PRODUCT 1?	.98
WHAT IS THE SALES PRICE OF PRODUCT 2?	3.75
WHAT IS THE VARIABLE COST OF PRODUCT 2?	2.17
WHAT IS THE SALES PRICE OF PRODUCT 3?	4.98
WHAT IS THE VARIABLE COST OF PRODUCT 3?	3.72
WHAT IS THE SALES PRICE OF PRODUCT 4?	5.39
WHAT IS THE VARIABLE COST OF PRODUCT 4?	4.01
WHAT ARE THE FIXED COSTS?	11000

At this point, the screen will clear and the TI will provide the answer:

NET INCOME = $2065

Try the program again, raising the variable costs, and watch how net income goes down. If you reduce the fixed costs, you'll see that net income goes up. You can run the program for any combination of product mix, fixed costs, and tax rate to determine the ultimate effect on net income.

TABLE 3.1
Selling Prices and Variable Costs
Baker Manufacturing Company

Product	Price	Variable Cost
1	$1.25	$0.98
2	3.75	2.17
3	4.98	3.72
4	5.39	4.01

FORMULA

The formula is included in the program listing; it is reviewed here for ease of reference.

NET INCOME

$$NI = (S - (FC + VC))*(1 - TR) \quad \text{(see program line 440)}$$

where

NI = net income
S = sales
FC = fixed costs
VC = variable costs
TR = tax rate

PROGRAM LISTING

COST-VOLUME-PROFIT ANALYSIS

```
100 CALL CLEAR
110 DIM Q(20),VCPU(20),SPPU(20)
120 PRINT "HOW MANY PRODUCTS ARE"
130 PRINT "IN THE PRODUCT LINE";
140 INPUT N
150 FOR I=1 TO N
160 PRINT
170 PRINT "HOW MANY UNITS OF PRODUCT";I
```

Note: If using the TI Professional Computer, substitute PRINT CHR$(12) for CALL CLEAR.

```
180 PRINT "ARE THERE";
190 INPUT Q(I)
200 NEXT I
210 PRINT
220 PRINT
230 PRINT "WHAT IS THE TAX RATE";
240 INPUT TR
250 CALL CLEAR
260 S=0
270 VC=0
280 FOR I=1 TO N
290 PRINT
300 PRINT "WHAT IS THE SALES PRICE"
310 PRINT "OF PRODUCT"; I;
320 INPUT SPPU(I)
330 S=Q(I)*SPPU*(I)+S
340 PRINT
350 PRINT "WHAT IS THE VARIABLE"
360 PRINT "COST OF PRODUCT";I;
370 INPUT VCPU(I)
380 VC=Q(I)*VCPU(I)+VC
390 NEXT I
400 PRINT
410 PRINT "WHAT ARE THE"
420 PRINT "FIXED COSTS";
430 INPUT FC
440 NI=(S-(FC+VC))*(1-TR)
450 CALL CLEAR
460 PRINT "NET INCOME=$";NI
470 PRINT
480 PRINT
490 PRINT
500 END
```

Pro Forma Financial Forecasting Analysis
4

One of the most important things financial analysts do is to predict future financial needs. When the sales department of a business makes a sales forecast, the company must determine what will be required to support the anticipated sales level. If sales are to increase, additional funds will be necessary to support the higher sales level.

THE FOUR-STEP PROCEDURE

Pro forma financial forecasting analysis is used for this purpose. The approach of the analysis is straightforward:

1. Each element of the previous year's balance sheet is examined to see if it is proportional to sales. If a given element is *not*, the amount in the account is not changed and is carried forward to the pro forma balance sheet. If the account will vary with sales, the amount in the account will be modified as explained in the next step.

2. Each element of the previous year's balance sheet that varies with sales is expressed as a percent of the previous year's sales. For example, if sales for the previous year were $1,000,000 and the cash account was $50,000, then the cash account would be expressed as 5 percent of sales. We then multiply the next year's projected sales by this factor to determine the amount in the account.

3. Any changes to retained earnings are posted to the pro forma balance sheet.

4. The liabilities and equities of the pro forma balance sheet are subtracted from the assets of the pro forma balance sheet. The difference equals the additional funds needed to support the desired sales increase.

The most difficult part of the process described is determining whether each of the accounts on the balance sheet will vary directly with sales. In some cases this will be easy. For instance, cash and accounts receivable will almost always react to changes in the sales level. If sales increase, more cash will be necessary to support ongoing operations. Accounts receivable will grow similarly. But what about the other accounts?

Let's consider the property, plant, and equipment account. If existing facilities have excess capacity (adequate to support the planned sales increase), the account will not vary with sales. Suppose the company's facilities are operating at capacity, though; further suppose that the plant has no room for additional equipment, and that there is no room on the property to build an additional plant. In that case, any planned increase in sales will require additional property, plant, and equipment; the property, plant, and equipment account will vary accordingly.

Making these determinations often requires considerable insight into the nature of the business, and how each account varies with sales. Let's assume we have that knowledge for the Baker Grain Company, the subject of our example on pro forma financial forecasting analysis.

SAMPLE ANALYSIS: COSTS OF SUPPORTING SALES INCREASE

Baker Grain Company processes and sells various kinds of feedstock and seed to farms. Last year, sales were $472,000. Next year, Baker plans for sales to reach $950,000. The company's balance sheet is shown in Table 4.1.

From past experience, we know that the cash, accounts receivable, inventory, accounts payable, and accrued wages and taxes accounts will vary directly with sales. The present facilities are not being utilized to capacity, and will support the planned sales increase. The other accounts will not vary with sales, either. During the year, Baker plans to add $70,000 to retained earnings.

Baker wants to know how much additional funding will be required to support the planned sales increase. To find the answer, let's run the Pro Forma Financial Forecasting Analysis program (the listing begins on page 32). Load

TABLE 4.1
Baker Grain Company
Balance Sheet for Year Ending December 31

Assets	
Cash	$50,000
Accounts Receivable	135,000
Inventory	346,000
Total Current Assets	$531,000
Property, Plant, and Equipment	2,234,000
Total Assets	$2,765,000
Liabilities and Equities	
Accounts Payable	$78,000
Notes Payable	15,000
Accrued Wages and Taxes	47,000
Total Current Liabilities	$140,000
Long-Term Debt	250,000
Total Liabilities	$390,000
Common Stock	$1,500,000
Preferred Stock	500,000
Retained Earnings	375,000
Total Liabilities and Equities	$2,765,000

the program into your TI-99/4A, enter the command RUN, and here's what the computer will ask for:

Computer Request	Operator Input
WHAT IS THE NAME OF THE COMPANY?	BAKER GRAIN COMPANY
WHAT WERE SALES IN THE LAST YEAR?	472000
WHAT SALES LEVEL IS DESIRED NEXT YEAR?	950000
HOW MANY ENTRIES ARE ON THE BALANCE SHEET FOR ASSETS?	4
FOR LIABILITIES?	4
FOR EQUITIES?	3
WHAT IS THE DESCRIPTOR FOR EACH LINE (INPUT RETAINED EARNINGS LAST—EVEN IF THIS IS A ZERO BALANCE ACCOUNT)	

Computer Request	Operator Input
?	CASH
?	ACCOUNTS RECEIVABLE
?	INVENTORY
?	PLANT AND EQUIPMENT
?	ACCOUNTS PAYABLE
?	NOTES PAYABLE
?	ACCRUED WAGES AND TAXES
?	LONG-TERM DEBT
?	COMMON STOCK
?	PREFERRED STOCK
?	RETAINED EARNINGS
WHAT IS THE AMOUNT FOR CASH FOR LAST YEAR?	50000
WILL THIS AMOUNT INCREASE WHEN SALES INCREASE (INPUT YES OR NO)?	YES
WHAT IS THE AMOUNT FOR ACCOUNTS RECEIVABLE FOR LAST YEAR?	135000
WILL THIS AMOUNT INCREASE WHEN SALES INCREASE (INPUT YES OR NO)?	YES
WHAT IS THE AMOUNT FOR INVENTORY FOR LAST YEAR?	346000
WILL THIS AMOUNT INCREASE WHEN SALES INCREASE (INPUT YES OR NO)?	YES
WHAT IS THE AMOUNT FOR PLANT AND EQUIPMENT FOR LAST YEAR?	2234000
WILL THIS AMOUNT INCREASE WHEN SALES INCREASE (INPUT YES OR NO)?	NO

Berk & Berk: Financial Analysis with Texas Instruments Microcomputers (Chilton)

Computer Request	Operator Input
WHAT IS THE AMOUNT FOR ACCOUNTS PAYABLE FOR LAST YEAR?	78000
WILL THIS AMOUNT INCREASE WHEN SALES INCREASE (INPUT YES OR NO)?	YES
WHAT IS THE AMOUNT FOR NOTES PAYABLE FOR LAST YEAR?	15000
WILL THIS AMOUNT INCREASE WHEN SALES INCREASE (INPUT YES OR NO)?	NO
WHAT IS THE AMOUNT FOR ACCRUED WAGES AND TAXES FOR LAST YEAR?	47000
WILL THIS AMOUNT INCREASE WHEN SALES INCREASE (INPUT YES OR NO)?	YES
WHAT IS THE AMOUNT FOR LONG-TERM DEBT FOR LAST YEAR?	250000
WILL THIS AMOUNT INCREASE WHEN SALES INCREASE (INPUT YES OR NO)?	NO
WHAT IS THE AMOUNT FOR COMMON STOCK FOR LAST YEAR?	1500000
WILL THIS AMOUNT INCREASE WHEN SALES INCREASE (INPUT YES OR NO)?	NO
WHAT IS THE AMOUNT FOR PREFERRED STOCK FOR LAST YEAR?	500000

Computer Request	Operator Input
WILL THIS AMOUNT INCREASE WHEN SALES INCREASE (INPUT YES OR NO)?	NO
WHAT IS THE AMOUNT FOR RETAINED EARNINGS FOR LAST YEAR?	375000
WILL THIS AMOUNT INCREASE WHEN SALES INCREASE (INPUT YES OR NO)?	NO
HOW MUCH MONEY WILL BE ADDED TO RETAINED EARNINGS?	70000

At this point, the screen will clear, and the computer will display the following information:

```
THIS IS THE PRO FORMA
BALANCE SHEET FOR
BAKER GRAIN COMPANY
FOR SALES OF $950000
              ASSETS
CASH =
$100635.59

ACCOUNTS RECEIVABLE =
$271716.10

INVENTORY =
$696398.31

PLANT AND EQUIPMENT =
$2234000.00

PRESS ENTER TO CONTINUE
?
```

(press enter, the screen will clear, and you'll see . . .)

```
            LIABILITIES
ACCOUNTS PAYABLE =
$156991.53

NOTES PAYABLE =
$15000.00
```

ACCRUED WAGES AND TAXES =
$94597.46

LONG-TERM DEBT =
$250000.00

PRESS ENTER TO CONTINUE
?

 (press enter, the screen will clear, and you'll see ...)

EQUITIES

COMMON STOCK =
$1500000

PREFERRED STOCK =
$500000

RETAINED EARNINGS =
$445000

PRESS ENTER TO CONTINUE
?

 (press enter, the screen will clear, and you'll see ...)

TOTAL FUNDS AVAILABLE =
$2961588.98

ADDITIONAL FUNDS NEEDED =
$341161.02

DONE

With this information, Baker can see that an additional $341,161.02 will be needed to support the planned sales increase.

FORMULAS

The formulas are included in the Program Listing, and are reviewed here for ease of reference.

PROJECTED ACCOUNT INCREASE

$$NYA = LYA * S2/S1 \quad \text{(see program line 570)}$$

where

NYA = balance required in next year's account
LYA = balance in last year's account
$S2$ = next year's sales
$S1$ = last year's sales

ADDITIONAL FUNDS NEEDED

$$AFN = SUA - (SUL + SUE) \quad \text{(see program line 1110)}$$

where

AFN = additional funds needed to support desired sales increase
SUA = sum of projected assets necessary to support desired sales level
SUL = sum of liabilities necessary to support desired sales level
SUE = sum of equities necessary to support desired sales level

PROGRAM LISTING

PRO FORMA FINANCIAL FORECASTING ANALYSIS

```
100 CALL CLEAR
110 DIM LI$(20),A2(20)
120 PRINT "WHAT IS THE NAME"
130 PRINT "OF THE COMPANY";
140 INPUT A$
150 PRINT
160 PRINT "WHAT WERE SALES"
170 PRINT "IN THE LAST YEAR";
180 INPUT S1
190 PRINT
200 PRINT "WHAT SALES LEVEL"
210 PRINT "IS DESIRED NEXT YEAR";
220 INPUT S2
230 PRINT
240 PRINT "HOW MANY ENTRIES ARE"
250 PRINT "ON THE BALANCE SHEET"
260 PRINT "FOR ASSETS";
270 INPUT AL
280 PRINT
290 PRINT "FOR LIABILITIES";
300 INPUT LL
```

Note: If using the TI Professional Computer, substitute PRINT CHR$(12) for CALL CLEAR.

```
310 PRINT
320 PRINT "FOR EQUITIES";
330 INPUT EL
340 CALL CLEAR
350 PRINT "WHAT IS THE DESCRIPTOR"
360 PRINT "FOR EACH LINE"
370 PRINT "(INPUT RETAINED EARNINGS"
380 PRINT "LAST—EVEN IF THIS IS"
390 PRINT "A ZERO BALANCE ACCOUNT)"
400 FOR I=1 TO AL+LL+EL
410 INPUT LI$(I)
420 NEXT I
430 CALL CLEAR
440 FOR I=1 TO AL+LL+EL
450 PRINT "WHAT IS THE AMOUNT FOR"
460 PRINT LI$(I)
470 PRINT "FOR LAST YEAR";
480 INPUT A2(I)
490 PRINT
500 PRINT "WILL THIS AMOUNT"
510 PRINT "INCREASE WHEN SALES"
520 PRINT "INCREASE"
530 PRINT "(INPUT YES OR NO)";
540 INPUT D$
550 PRINT
560 IF D$="NO" THEN 580
570 A2(I)=A2(I)*S2/S1
580 NEXT I
590 PRINT "HOW MUCH MONEY"
600 PRINT "WILL BE ADDED TO"
610 PRINT "RETAINED EARNINGS";
620 INPUT ARE
630 A2(AL+LL+EL)=A2(AL+LL+EL)+ARE
640 CALL CLEAR
650 PRINT "THIS IS THE PRO-FORMA"
660 PRINT "BALANCE SHEET FOR"
670 PRINT A$
680 PRINT "FOR SALES OF $";S2
690 PRINT
700 PRINT
710 PRINT TAB(10);"ASSETS"
720 PRINT
730 FOR I=1 TO AL
740 PRINT LI$(I);" = "
750 PRINT "$";INT(A2(I)+.005)*100)/100
760 PRINT
770 SUA=SUA+A2(I)
```

```
780 NEXT I
790 PRINT "PRESS ENTER TO CONTINUE"
800 INPUT B$
810 CALL CLEAR
820 PRINT TAB(10);"LIABILITIES"
830 PRINT
840 FOR I=AL+1 TO AL+LL
850 PRINT LI$(I);" ="
860 PRINT "$";INT((A2(I)+.005)*100)/100
870 PRINT
880 SUL=SUL+A2(I)
890 NEXT I
900 PRINT
910 PRINT "PRESS ENTER TO CONTINUE"
920 INPUT B$
930 CALL CLEAR
940 PRINT TAB(10);"EQUITIES"
950 PRINT
960 FOR I=AL+LL+1 TO AL+LL+EL
970 PRINT LI$(I);" ="
980 PRINT "$";INT((A2(I)+.005)*100)/100
990 PRINT
1000 SUE=SUE+A2(I)
1010 NEXT I
1020 PRINT
1030 PRINT "PRESS ENTER TO CONTINUE"
1040 INPUT B$
1050 CALL CLEAR
1060 PRINT "TOTAL FUNDS AVAILABLE="
1070 PRINT "$";INT((SUL+SUE+.005)*100)/100
1080 PRINT
1090 PRINT
1100 PRINT "ADDITIONAL FUNDS NEEDED="
1110 PRINT "$";INT(SUA-(SUL+SUE)+.005)*100)/100
1120 PRINT
1130 PRINT
1140 PRINT
1150 END
```

Cost of Capital Analysis
5

One of the most important considerations for any business is its cost of capital, or how much it has to pay for the money it uses. For a small business with only one source of financing, this information is readily available. For large corporations, however, determining the cost of capital is much more complex: such companies are typically financed through a combination of various stock offerings, debt, and the use of retained earnings. Each of these has a different cost. Finding the combined cost of all sources of capital is critically important to a business, since without this knowledge there is no way to accurately gauge the feasibility of new projects.

FIVE COST CATEGORIES FOR EXAMINATION

When corporations assess their cost of capital, they generally address five areas:
1. The current capital structure
2. The current cost of capital
3. The marginal cost of obtaining new capital
4. The resulting capital structure
5. The resulting overall cost of capital

Let's examine each of these concepts; then we'll illustrate how to find each with a cost of capital analysis program.

CURRENT CAPITAL STRUCTURE

As mentioned, corporations are usually funded through a combination of retained earnings, common stock, preferred stock, and debt. *Current capital structure* refers to the percentage of each form of financing that makes up the corporation's total available capital. For example, a corporation's capital structure may consist of 10 percent retained earnings, 30 percent common stock, 15 percent preferred stock, and 45 percent debt.

CURRENT COST OF CAPITAL

Once a corporation's current capital structure is known, we will next want to know the corporation's overall cost of capital. To find the current cost of all forms of capital used by the corporation, the computer will first find the cost of each component of the capital structure. Then it will calculate a weighted average of all the components to determine the *current cost of capital*.

MARGINAL COST OF CAPITAL

Once a corporation knows its cost of capital, it will want to determine the marginal cost of capital for new projects. The marginal cost of capital is the cost of additional financing. If the corporation has enough funds available to take on new projects without turning to outside sources, the marginal cost of capital will be the same as the current cost of capital. This is usually not the case, though, because most businesses have to rely on outside financing in order to undertake new projects.

When a corporation seeks additional financing, it will either stay with its current capital structure (i.e., obtain financing in the same proportion as the current capital structure), or it will deviate from its current capital structure. Regardless of the financial decision, the cost of additional financing will most likely be different from the current cost of capital. That's because the new financing will probably involve flotation costs for new stock, and new debt will probably have a different cost from old debt. The cost of obtaining this new financing is called the *marginal cost of capital*.

RESULTING CAPITAL STRUCTURE

If a business decides to stay with its existing capital structure when raising new sources of financing, then by definition the *resulting capital structure* is the same as the old capital structure. There are a variety of reasons why a company might want to stay within its existing capital structure. Most involve ceilings imposed on the debt ratio by outside influences (such as bond-rating agencies), or internal analyses that lead the business to believe the current capital structure best satisfies its financial needs. If the corporation selects sources of financing in a proportion different from the current capital structure, the resulting capital structure will be different from the original one.

RESULTING OVERALL COST OF CAPITAL

After the corporation has obtained additional financing, it will have a new overall cost of capital, even if it opted to stay with the existing capital structure. The resulting overall cost of capital will be a function of the amount and cost of the old capital and the amount and cost of the new capital.

Now that we have an understanding of the intricacies involved in computing the cost of capital, we're ready to tackle a problem.

SAMPLE ANALYSIS: DEVELOPING NEW PRODUCT

The balance sheet for Quantel Microprocessors, Inc., is shown in Table 5.1.

Quantel wants to begin development of a new microprocessor, but the project will require an additional $2,000,000. Quantel is unsure how to raise the necessary capital. The company's current cost of debt is 10 percent, but new

TABLE 5.1
Quantel, Inc.
Balance Sheet for the Year Ending December 31

Assets	
Cash	$50,000
Accounts Receivable	780,000
Inventory	2,000,000
Total Current Assets	$2,830,000
Property, Plant, and Equipment	3,000,000
Total Assets	$5,830,000
Liabilities and Equities	
Debt	$1,000,000
Total Debt	1,000,000
Common Stock	2,500,000
Preferred Stock	2,000,000
Retained Earnings	330,000
Total Liabilities and Equity	$5,830,000

debt will cost 14 percent. Issuing either common or preferred stock will involve a flotation cost of 13 percent of the value of the stock. Quantel's common stock is currently selling at $50.00 per share, with an annual dividend of $7.00. The company's securities analysis department predicts that the price of the stock will increase $4.00 during the next year. Quantel's preferred stock is selling at $100.00 per share, with an annual dividend of $12.50.

Quantel wants to know what the existing cost of capital is, and what the new cost of capital will be if it: (a) keeps the existing capital structure; or (b) raises all the money by selling bonds (i.e., using new debt).

Let's use the Cost of Capital Analysis program to answer these questions. Load the program (the listing begins on page 45, enter the command RUN, and here's what the computer will ask for:

Computer Request	Operator Input
WHAT IS THE TOTAL DOLLAR AMOUNT OF EXISTING COMMON STOCK?	2500000
WHAT IS THE ANNUAL DIVIDEND OF THE STOCK?	7
WHAT IS THE MARKET PRICE OF THE COMMON STOCK?	50
WHAT IS THE EXPECTED CAPITAL GAIN (IN DOLLARS)?	4
WHAT IS THE DOLLAR AMOUNT OF EXISTING PREFERRED STOCK?	2000000
WHAT IS THE ANNUAL DIVIDEND FOR THE PREFERRED STOCK?	12.50
WHAT IS THE MARKET PRICE OF THE PREFERRED STOCK?	100
WHAT IS THE TOTAL DOLLAR AMOUNT OF EXISTING RETAINED EARNINGS?	330000
WHAT IS THE TOTAL DOLLAR AMOUNT OF THE EXISTING DEBT?	1000000

Computer Request	Operator Input
WHAT IS THE COST OF THIS DEBT (EXPRESSED AS A PERCENT)?	10
WHAT IS THE COMPANY'S TAX RATE (EXPRESSED AS A PERCENT)?	50

At this point, the screen will clear, and the computer will display the company's present capital structure:

```
PRESENT CAPITAL STRUCTURE
    48.54 PERCENT COMMON STOCK
    34.31 PERCENT PREFERRED
          STOCK
    17.15 PERCENT DEBT
WEIGHTED AVERAGE
COST OF CAPITAL
= 15.83 PERCENT
PRESS ENTER TO CONTINUE
?
```

(press enter, the screen will clear, and you'll see . . .)

Computer Request	Operator Input
DO YOU WANT TO RAISE ADDITIONAL CAPITAL (INPUT YES OR NO)?	YES
HOW MUCH MORE DO YOU WISH TO RAISE (IN DOLLARS)?	2000000
DO YOU WISH TO KEEP THE SAME CAPITAL STRUCTURE (INPUT YES OR NO)?	YES
WHAT IS THE FLOTATION COST FOR THE COMMON STOCK (EXPRESSED AS A PERCENT)?	13

Computer Request	Operator Input
WHAT IS THE FLOTATION COST FOR THE PREFERRED STOCK (EXPRESSED AS A PERCENT)?	13
WHAT IS THE COST OF THE NEW DEBT (EXPRESSED AS A PERCENT)?	14

At this point, the screen will clear, and the following information will be displayed:

THE COST OF
NEWLY RAISED CAPITAL IS
17.82 PERCENT

THE NEW TOTAL
WEIGHTED AVERAGE
COST OF CAPITAL
(INCORPORATING THE
NEWLY RAISED CAPITAL) IS
16.34 PERCENT

PRESS ENTER TO CONTINUE
?

(press enter, the screen will clear, and you'll see . . .)

THE NEW CAPITAL
STRUCTURE IS

    48.54 PERCENT COMMON STOCK
    34.31 PERCENT PREFERRED
        STOCK
    17.15 PERCENT DEBT

** DONE **

Quantel now knows the marginal cost of new capital will be 17.82 percent if they keep their existing capital structure. The new weighted average cost of all Quantel's capital (after the $2,000,000 has been raised) will be 16.34 percent. The capital structure after raising the additional funds is the same as it was before, since that's how we specified the problem.

Quantel is only halfway through the problem, though. The company also wants to know the marginal cost of capital, the new average cost of capital, and the new capital structure if they raise all of the required additional financing through the issuance of bonds. Let's run the program again to see what the new answer is:

Computer Request	Operator Input
WHAT IS THE TOTAL DOLLAR AMOUNT OF EXISTING COMMON STOCK?	2500000
WHAT IS THE ANNUAL DIVIDEND OF THE COMMON STOCK?	7
WHAT IS THE MARKET PRICE OF THE COMMON STOCK?	50
WHAT IS THE EXPECTED CAPITAL GAIN (IN DOLLARS)?	4
WHAT IS THE DOLLAR AMOUNT OF EXISTING PREFERRED STOCK?	2000000
WHAT IS THE ANNUAL DIVIDEND FOR THE PREFERRED STOCK?	12.50
WHAT IS THE MARKET PRICE OF THE PREFERRED STOCK?	100
WHAT IS THE TOTAL DOLLAR AMOUNT OF EXISTING RETAINED EARNINGS?	330000
WHAT IS THE TOTAL DOLLAR AMOUNT OF THE EXISTING DEBT?	1000000
WHAT IS THE COST OF THIS DEBT (EXPRESSED AS A PERCENT)?	10
WHAT IS THE COMPANY'S TAX RATE (EXPRESSED AS A PERCENT)?	50

At this point, the screen will clear and we'll see the same capital structure as when we ran the problem last time. Remember, this is the company's current capital structure:

PRESENT CAPITAL STRUCTURE
    48.54 PERCENT COMMON STOCK
    34.31 PERCENT PREFERRED
        STOCK
    17.15 PERCENT DEBT

WEIGHTED AVERAGE
COST OF CAPITAL
= 15.83 PERCENT

PRESS ENTER TO CONTINUE
?

(press enter, the screen will clear, and you'll see . . .)

Computer Request	Operator Input
DO YOU WISH TO RAISE ADDITIONAL CAPITAL (INPUT YES OR NO)?	YES
HOW MUCH MORE DO YOU WISH TO RAISE (IN DOLLARS)?	2000000
DO YOU WISH TO KEEP THE SAME CAPITAL STRUCTURE (INPUT YES OR NO)?	NO
WHAT IS THE FLOTATION COST FOR THE COMMON STOCK (EXPRESSED AS A PERCENT)?	0
WHAT IS THE FLOTATION COST FOR THE PREFERRED STOCK (EXPRESSED AS A PERCENT)?	0

(remember, we're not going to issue any stock this time!!)

WHAT IS THE COST OF THE NEW DEBT (EXPRESSED AS A PERCENT)?	14

Computer Request	Operator Input
WHAT PERCENT OF NEW FUNDS IS FROM COMMON STOCK?	0
WHAT PERCENT OF NEW FUNDS IS FROM PREFERRED STOCK?	0

At this point, the screen will clear and the computer will display:

THE COST OF THE
NEWLY RAISED CAPITAL IS
7 PERCENT

    (remember, this is the after-tax cost)

THE NEW TOTAL
WEIGHTED AVERAGE
COST OF CAPITAL
(INCORPORATING THE
NEWLY RAISED CAPITAL) IS
13.57 PERCENT

PRESS ENTER TO CONTINUE
?

    (after pressing enter, the computer will display the new capital structure . . .)

THE NEW CAPITAL
STRUCTURE IS

    36.14 PERCENT COMMON STOCK
    25.54 PERCENT PREFERRED
        STOCK
    38.31 PERCENT DEBT

** DONE **

Having run the analysis both ways, Quantel can see that raising the new funds through the use of debt at 14 percent will present a lower marginal cost of capital, as well as lower the company's overall cost of capital. If the company doesn't have a ceiling on the percentage of debt it is allowed to carry (or if it is not exceeding such a ceiling if one does exist), it should opt for changing its capital structure and raising the required additional financing entirely through the use of debt.

FORMULAS

The formulas are included in the Program Listing, and are reviewed here only for ease of reference.

COST OF COMMON STOCK

$$KC = D/PC + CG \quad \text{(see program lines 330 and 1410)}$$

where

KC = cost of common stock
D = annual dividend of common stock
PC = market price of common stock
CG = expected growth of common stock

COST OF PREFERRED STOCK

$$KP = DP/PP \quad \text{(see program lines 500 and 1420)}$$

where

KP = cost of preferred stock
DP = annual dividend of preferred stock
PP = market price of preferred stock

THE COST OF DEBT

$$KDAT = KD*(1 - T) \quad \text{(see program lines 760 and 1400)}$$

where

$KDAT$ = cost of debt after taxes
KD = cost of debt before taxes
T = tax rate

WEIGHTED AVERAGE COST OF CAPITAL

$$WACC = PCCS*KC + PCPS*KP + PCDT*KD$$
(see program lines 770-810, 1470, and 1620-1630)

where

$WACC$ = weighted average cost of capital
$PCCS$ = percent common stock

KC = cost of common stock
$PCPS$ = percent preferred stock
KP = cost of preferred stock
$PCDT$ = percent debt
KD = cost of debt

PROGRAM LISTING

COST OF CAPITAL ANALYSIS

```
100 CALL CLEAR
110 PRINT "WHAT IS THE TOTAL"
120 PRINT "DOLLAR AMOUNT OF"
130 PRINT "EXISTING COMMON"
140 PRINT "STOCK";
150 INPUT CS
160 IF CS=0 THEN 350
170 PRINT
180 PRINT "WHAT IS THE ANNUAL"
190 PRINT "DIVIDEND OF THE"
200 PRINT "COMMON STOCK";
210 INPUT D
220 PRINT
230 PRINT "WHAT IS THE MARKET"
240 PRINT "PRICE OF THE COMMON"
250 PRINT "STOCK";
260 INPUT PC
270 PRINT
280 PRINT "WHAT IS THE EXPECTED"
290 PRINT "CAPITAL GAIN"
300 PRINT "(IN DOLLARS)";
310 INPUT CG
320 CG=CG/PC
330 KC=D/PC+CG
340 PRINT
350 PRINT "WHAT IS THE DOLLAR"
360 PRINT "AMOUNT OF EXISTING"
370 PRINT "PREFERRED STOCK";
380 INPUT PS
390 IF PS=0 THEN 520
400 PRINT
410 PRINT "WHAT IS THE ANNUAL"
420 PRINT "DIVIDEND FOR THE"
430 PRINT "PREFERRED STOCK";
```

Note: If using the TI Professional Computer, substitute PRINT CHR$(12) for CALL CLEAR.

```
440 INPUT DP
450 PRINT
460 PRINT "WHAT IS THE MARKET"
470 PRINT "PRICE OF THE"
480 PRINT "PREFERRED STOCK";
490 INPUT PP
500 KP=DP/PP
510 PRINT
520 PRINT "WHAT IS THE TOTAL"
530 PRINT "DOLLAR AMOUNT OF EXISTING"
540 PRINT "RETAINED EARNINGS";
550 INPUT RE
560 PRINT
570 PRINT "WHAT IS THE TOTAL"
580 PRINT "DOLLAR AMOUNT OF"
590 PRINT "THE EXISTING DEBT";
600 INPUT DT
610 PRINT
620 IF DT=0 THEN 770
630 PRINT "WHAT IS THE COST"
640 PRINT "OF THIS DEBT"
650 PRINT "(EXPRESSED AS A"
660 PRINT "PERCENT)";
670 INPUT KD
680 KD=KD/100
690 PRINT
700 PRINT "WHAT IS THE COMPANY'S"
710 PRINT "TAX RATE"
720 PRINT "(EXPRESSED AS A"
730 PRINT "PERCENT)";
740 INPUT T
750 T=T/100
760 KD=KD*(1-T)
770 TF=CS+PS+RE+DT
780 PCCS=(CS+RE)/TF
790 PCPS=PS/TF
800 PCDT=DT/TF
810 WACC=PCCS*KC+PCPS*KP+PCDT*KD
820 CALL CLEAR
830 PRINT "PRESENT CAPITAL STRUCTURE"
840 PRINT
850 PRINT
860 PRINT INT(PCCS+.00005)*10000)/100;
" PERCENT COMMON STOCK"
870 PRINT
880 PRINT INT((PCPS+.00005)*10000)/100;
" PERCENT PREFERRED"
```

```
890 PRINT TAB(10);"STOCK"
900 PRINT
910 PRINT INT((PCDT+.00005)*10000)/100;
" PERCENT DEBT"
920 PRINT
930 PRINT
940 PRINT "WEIGHTED AVERAGE"
950 PRINT "COST OF CAPITAL"
960 PRINT "=";INT ((WACC+.00005)*10000)/100;" PERCENT"
970 PRINT
980 PRINT
990 PRINT "PRESS ENTER TO CONTINUE"
1000 INPUT B$
1010 CALL CLEAR
1020 PRINT "DO YOU WISH TO"
1030 PRINT "RAISE ADDITIONAL CAPITAL"
1040 "(INPUT YES OR NO)";
1050 INPUT AN$
1060 IF AN$="NO" THEN 1910
1070 PRINT
1080 PRINT "HOW MUCH MORE"
1090 PRINT "DO YOU WISH TO RAISE"
1100 PRINT "(IN DOLLARS)";
1110 INPUT AMT
1120 CALL CLEAR
1130 PRINT "DO YOU WISH TO"
1140 PRINT "KEEP THE SAME"
1150 PRINT "CAPITAL STRUCTURE"
1160 PRINT "(INPUT YES OR NO)";
1170 INPUT AN$
1180 PRINT
1190 PRINT "WHAT IS THE"
1200 PRINT "FLOTATION COST FOR"
1210 PRINT "THE COMMON STOCK"
1220 PRINT "(EXPRESSED AS A"
1230 PRINT "PERCENT)";
1240 INPUT FCCS
1250 FCCS=FCCS/100
1260 PRINT
1270 PRINT "WHAT IS THE"
1280 PRINT "FLOTATION COST FOR"
1290 PRINT "THE PREFERRED STOCK"
1300 PRINT "(EXPRESSED AS A"
1310 PRINT "PERCENT)";
1320 INPUT FCPS
1330 FCPS=FCPS/100
1340 PRINT
```

```
1350 PRINT "WHAT IS THE COST"
1360 PRINT "OF THE NEW DEBT"
1370 PRINT "(EXPRESSED AS A"
1380 PRINT "PERCENT)";
1390 INPUT KND
1400 KND=KND*(1-T)/100
1410 KNC=D/(PC*(1-FCCS))+CG
1420 KNP=DP/(PP*(1-FCPS))
1430 NPCCS=PCCS
1440 NPCPS=PCPS
1450 NPCDT=PCDT
1460 IF AN$="NO" THEN 1490
1470 NWACC=NPCCS*KNC+NPCPS*KNP+NPCDT*KND
1480 GO TO 1630
1490 PRINT
1500 PRINT "WHAT PERCENT OF NEW"
1510 PRINT "FUNDS IS FROM"
1520 PRINT "COMMON STOCK";
1530 INPUT NPCCS
1540 PRINT
1550 NPCCS=NPCCS/100
1560 PRINT "WHAT PERCENT OF NEW"
1570 PRINT "FUNDS IS FROM"
1580 PRINT "PREFERRED STOCK";
1590 INPUT NPCPS
1600 NPCPS=NPCPS/100
1610 NPCDT=1-(NPCPS+NPCCS)
1620 NWACC=NPCCS*KNC+NPCPS*KNP+NPCDT*KND
1630 TOTWACC=WACC*(TF/(TF+AMT))+NWACC*(AMT/(TE+AMT))
1640 CALL CLEAR
1650 PRINT "THE COST OF THE"
1660 PRINT "NEWLY RAISED CAPITAL IS"
1670 PRINT INT((NWACC+.00005)*10000)/100;
" PERCENT"
1680 PRINT
1690 PRINT "THE NEW TOTAL"
1700 PRINT "WEIGHTED AVERAGE"
1710 PRINT "COST OF CAPITAL"
1720 PRINT "(INCORPORATING THE"
1730 PRINT "NEWLY RAISED CAPITAL) IS"
1740 PRINT INT((TOTWACC+.00005)*10000)/100;"PERCENT"
1750 PCCS=(CS+RE+NPCCS*AMT)/(TF+AMT)
1760 PCPS=(PS+NPCPS*AMT)/(TF+AMT)
1770 PCDT=(DT+NPCDT*AMT)/(TF+AMT)
1780 PRINT
1790 PRINT "PRESS ENTER TO CONTINUE"
1800 INPUT B$
```

```
1810 CALL CLEAR
1820 PRINT "THE NEW CAPITAL"
1830 PRINT "STRUCTURE IS"
1840 PRINT
1850 PRINT INT((PCCS+.00005)*10000)/100;" PERCENT COMMON STOCK"
1860 PRINT
1870 PRINT INT((PCPS+.00005)*10000)/100;" PERCENT PREFERRED"
1880 PRINT TAB(10);"STOCK"
1890 PRINT
1900 PRINT INT((PCDT+.00005)*10000)/100;" PERCENT DEBT"
1910 END
```

Depreciation Analysis 6

Depreciation is the process of spreading the cost of an asset over its useful service life. When a business purchases an asset, the cost will reduce the income of the business. Since the asset will usually last longer than a year, some method must be used to spread the cost over the period of time the asset will provide a service. We'll examine four of the most popular methods in this chapter.

Depreciation is a significant factor in the financial affairs of a company, because the Internal Revenue Service has ruled that depreciation is a deductible expense, thereby reducing the amount of taxes a business must pay.

NORMAL DEPRECIATION

Normal depreciation spreads the cost equally over the asset's useful service life. The two methods of normal depreciation are the straight-line method and the units-of-production method.

STRAIGHT-LINE DEPRECIATION

In the straight-line method, the cost of the asset (minus its salvage value) is simply divided by its service life. The resulting quotient is the amount of depreciation for each year of the asset's service life.

UNITS-OF-PRODUCTION DEPRECIATION

The units-of-production method is slightly more complex than the straight-line method; it spreads the cost of the asset (minus its salvage value) over the total number of units that will be produced by the asset. The quotient is the depreciation per unit produced. The total number of units produced in each year is then multiplied by this number to determine the depreciation for that year. The units-of-production method can be used for machines that will produce a known number of units, or operate for a known number of hours, or be driven for a known number of miles.

ACCELERATED DEPRECIATION

As the name implies, in this category the amount of depreciation that may be charged against profits is accelerated, so that larger amounts may be recognized earlier in the service life of an asset. Businesses generally prefer to use accelerated depreciation methods, because these methods allow the business to pay reduced income taxes in the early stages of an asset's life. Later on, higher taxes will have to be paid. In effect, the use of accelerated depreciation defers taxes until the later years of an asset's life. That amounts to an interest-free loan to the business. Two methods of accelerated depreciation are the sum-of-the-years'-digits method and the declining balance method.

SUM-OF-THE-YEARS'-DEPRECIATION

The sum-of-the years'-digits method adds the numbers of each year in the asset's service life together, and then divides this number into the years of the asset's service life in reverse order. The resulting quotient for each year is then multiplied by the cost of the asset minus its salvage value. The process is really less complicated than it sounds. For example, let's consider an asset with a service life of three years, a cost of $8000, and a salvage value of $2,000. The sum of the years' digits is 6 (we obtained this by adding 1 + 2 + 3). The depreciation for the first year, then, would be:

$$\tfrac{3}{6}*(\$8000 - \$2000) = \$3000$$

Notice that half of the asset's total depreciation is deducted in the first year. This is considerably more than would be deducted using a normal depreciation method. That's why it's called accelerated depreciation.

We included this example just to give you a better feel for what the computer will be doing. You don't have to worry about doing the calculations, since your TI will handle them.

DECLINING BALANCE DEPRECIATION

The declining balance method usually doubles the rate of depreciation that would be used with the straight-line method, although for some assets, the rate of depreciation is increased by 50 percent (this is called 1½ declining balance depreciation). Depreciation for the first year is determined by multiplying the asset's value by the increased rate. Each succeeding year's depreciation is then calculated by: (1) Finding the difference between the asset's value for the previous year and the amount of depreciation claimed for that year; and then (2) multiplying this difference by the same increased depreciation rate.

Our program for depreciation analysis is set up so that the declining balance depreciation rate will always be double the normal rate (the listing begins on page 58). If you want to use the program to calculate 1½ declining balance depreciation, then you should change line 1010

    from: 1010 DEP=2/LAS
    to: 1010 DEP=1.5/LAS

SAMPLE ANALYSIS: DETERMINING BEST DEPRECIATION METHOD

Jack Starbuck bought a new motorcycle for use in his business. The motorcycle cost $6,000, and has a useful service life of three years. During that time, Mr. Starbuck anticipates accumulating 25,000 miles on the motorcycle, with 10,000 miles of use the first year, and 7,500 miles in each of the remaining years. At the end of this period, the motorcycle can be sold for $2,000.

Mr. Starbuck is doing his tax planning for the next three years. After consulting with his tax attorney, he learns that any one of the four methods we have reviewed here can be used in his particular business situation. Mr. Starbuck wants to compare how much depreciation is deductible each year, using each of the four depreciation methods.

Let's perform this comparison with a depreciation analysis. Load the program into your TI-99/4A (the listing begins on page 58), enter the command RUN, and here's what the computer will ask for:

Computer Request	Operator Input
WHAT IS THE ASSET YOU ARE DEPRECIATING?	MOTORCYCLE
WHAT IS THE INITIAL COST OF MOTORCYCLE?	6000
WHAT IS THE EXPECTED SALVAGE VALUE OF MOTORCYCLE?	2000
FOR HOW MANY YEARS DO YOU EXPECT SERVICE FROM MOTORCYCLE?	3
ENTER THE NUMBER CORRESPONDING TO THE DEPRECIATION METHOD YOU WISH TO USE	
1 FOR STRAIGHT LINE	
2 FOR UNITS OF PRODUCTION	
3 FOR DECLINING BALANCE	
4 FOR SUM-OF-THE YEARS'-DIGITS	
?	1

At this point, the screen will clear, and the computer will show the depreciation for each year using the straight-line method:

USING THE STRAIGHT LINE
METHOD THE DEPRECIATION
PER YEAR FOR MOTORCYCLE
IS $1333.33

PRESS ENTER TO CONTINUE
?

After you've pressed the enter key, the program will continue:

Computer Request	Operator Input
DO YOU WISH TO RUN THE PROGRAM AGAIN (INPUT YES OR NO)?	YES

Computer Request	Operator Input
ENTER THE NUMBER CORRESPONDING TO THE DEPRECIATION METHOD YOU WISH TO USE	

1 FOR STRAIGHT LINE
   2 FOR UNITS
      OF PRODUCTION
   3 FOR DECLINING BALANCE
   4 FOR SUM-OF-THE-
      YEARS'-DIGITS	

?	2
WHAT ARE THE UNITS THAT MOTORCYCLE IS PRODUCING?	MILES
WHAT ARE THE ESTIMATED MILES THAT MOTORCYCLE WILL PRODUCE?	25000

At this point, the screen will clear, and the computer will show the depreciation for each unit of production:

USING THE UNITS OF
PRODUCTION METHOD THE
DEPRECIATION FOR
MOTORCYCLE IS $.16
PER UNIT

Once the computer has shown the above information, it will go on to ask the anticipated usage for each year. After each input, the computer will show the depreciation for that year:

Computer Request	Operator Input
WHAT ARE THE EXPECTED MILES FOR YEAR 1?	10000
THE ANNUAL DEPRECIATION EXPENSE FOR YEAR 1 IS $1600	
WHAT ARE THE EXPECTED MILES FOR YEAR 2?	7500
THE ANNUAL DEPRECIATION EXPENSE FOR YEAR 2 IS $1200	

Computer Request	Operator Input
WHAT ARE THE EXPECTED MILES FOR YEAR 3?	7500

THE ANNUAL DEPRECIATION
EXPENSE FOR YEAR 3
IS $1200

PRESS ENTER TO CONTINUE
?

    (after you press enter, the program will continue...)

DO YOU WISH TO RUN THE PROGRAM AGAIN (INPUT YES OR NO)?	YES

ENTER THE NUMBER
CORRESPONDING TO THE
DEPRECIATION METHOD
YOU WISH TO USE

    1 FOR STRAIGHT LINE

    2 FOR UNITS
      OF PRODUCTION

    3 FOR DECLINING BALANCE

    4 FOR SUM-OF-THE-
      YEARS'-DIGITS

?   3

    At this point, the screen will clear, and the computer will show the depreciation for each year using the declining balance method:

USING THE DECLINING BALANCE
METHOD THE DEPRECIATION
FOR YEAR 1 IS $4000

PRESS ENTER TO CONTINUE
?

    (after you press enter, the program will continue...)

USING THE DECLINING BALANCE
METHOD THE DEPRECIATION
FOR YEAR 2 IS $ 0

PRESS ENTER TO CONTINUE
?

(after you press enter, the program will continue ...)

USING THE DECLINING BALANCE
METHOD THE DEPRECIATION
FOR YEAR 3 IS $ 0

PRESS ENTER TO CONTINUE
?

(after you press enter, the program will continue ...)

DO YOU WISH TO RUN
THE PROGRAM AGAIN
(INPUT YES OR NO)?   YES

ENTER THE NUMBER
CORRESPONDING TO THE
DEPRECIATION METHOD
YOU WISH TO USE

    1 FOR STRAIGHT LINE

    2 FOR UNITS
      OF PRODUCTION

    3 FOR DECLINING BALANCE

    4 FOR SUM-OF-THE-
      YEARS'-DIGITS

?   4

At this point, the screen will clear, and the computer will show the depreciation for each year using the sum-of-the-years'-digits method:

USING THE SUM-OF-THE-
YEARS'-DIGITS METHOD
THE ANNUAL DEPRECIATION
FOR YEAR 1 IS $2000

PRESS ENTER TO CONTINUE
?

(after you press enter, the program will continue ...)

USING THE SUM-OF-THE-
YEARS'-DIGITS METHOD
THE ANNUAL DEPRECIATION
FOR YEAR 2 IS $1333.33

PRESS ENTER TO CONTINUE
?

(after you press enter, the program will continue . . .)

```
USING THE SUM-OF-THE
YEARS'-DIGITS METHOD
THE ANNUAL DEPRECIATION
FOR YEAR 3 IS $666.67

PRESS ENTER TO CONTINUE
?
```

(after you press enter, the program will continue . . .)

```
DO YOU WISH TO RUN
THE PROGRAM AGAIN
(INPUT YES OR NO)?                    NO
** DONE **
```

We can see from the four sample analyses that the amount of depreciation Mr. Starbuck can claim will vary considerably, depending on the depreciation method selected. He has to examine his income situation and decide which method offers the best tax advantages.

FORMULAS

Formulas are included in the Program Listing; they are reviewed here for your reference.

STRAIGHT-LINE DEPRECIATION

$$DEP = (CAS - SAS)/LAS \quad \text{(see program line 520)}$$

where

DEP = annual depreciation
CAS = initial asset cost
SAS = asset salvage value
LAS = asset service life

UNITS OF PRODUCTION DEPRECIATION

$$DEP = (CAS - SAS)/UN \quad \text{(see program line 720)}$$

where

DEP = annual depreciation
CAS = initial asset cost
SAS = asset salvage value
UN = total number of units the asset will produce

DECLINING BALANCE DEPRECIATION

$$DEP = 2/LAS \quad \text{(see program line 1010)}$$

where

DEP = annual depreciation
LAS = asset service life

SUM-OF-THE-YEARS'-DIGITS DEPRECIATION

$$DEP = TEMP/SYD*(CAS - SAS)$$

(see program lines 1180 and 1210)

where

DEP = annual depreciation
$TEMP$ = number of years in reverse order
(e.g., for a five-year asset, TEMP = 5 at year 1, 4 at year 2, 3 at year 3, 2 at year 4, and 1 at year 5)
SYD = sum of the years' digits
CAS = initial asset cost
SAS = asset salvage value

PROGRAM LISTING

DEPRECIATION ANALYSIS

```
100 CALL CLEAR
110 PRINT "WHAT IS THE ASSET"
120 PRINT "YOU ARE"
130 PRINT "DEPRECIATING";
140 INPUT A$
150 PRINT
```

Note: If using the TI Professional Computer, substitute PRINT CHR$(12) for CALL CLEAR.

```
160 PRINT "WHAT IS THE INITIAL"
170 PRINT "COST OF ";AS$;
180 INPUT CAS
190 PRINT
200 PRINT "WHAT IS THE EXPECTED"
210 PRINT "SALVAGE VALUE"
220 PRINT "OF ";AS$;
230 INPUT SAS
240 PRINT
250 PRINT "FOR HOW MANY YEARS"
260 PRINT "DO YOU EXPECT SERVICE"
270 PRINT "FROM ";AS$;
280 INPUT LAS
290 CALL CLEAR
300 PRINT "ENTER THE NUMBER"
310 PRINT "CORRESPONDING TO THE"
320 PRINT "DEPRECIATION METHOD"
330 PRINT "YOU WISH TO USE"
340 PRINT
350 PRINT TAB(5);"1 FOR STRAIGHT LINE"
360 PRINT
370 PRINT TAB(5);"2 FOR UNITS"
380 PRINT TAB(10);"OF PRODUCTION"
390 PRINT
400 PRINT TAB(5);"3 FOR DECLINING BALANCE"
410 PRINT
420 PRINT TAB(5);"4 FOR SUM-OF-THE-"
430 PRINT TAB(10);"YEARS' DIGITS"
440 PRINT
450 INPUT AN
460 CALL CLEAR
470 IF AN=1 THEN 520
480 IF AN=2 THEN 620
490 IF AN=3 THEN 1010
500 IF AN=4 THEN 1180
510 GO TO 290
520 DEP=(CAS-SAS)/LAS
530 DEP=INT((DEP+.005)*100)/100
540 PRINT "USING THE STRAIGHT LINE"
550 PRINT "METHOD THE DEPRECIATION"
560 PRINT "PER YEAR FOR ";AS$
570 PRINT "IS $";DEP
580 PRINT
590 PRINT "PRESS ENTER TO CONTINUE"
600 INPUT B$
610 GO TO 1320
620 PRINT "WHAT ARE THE UNITS"
```

```
630 PRINT "THAT ";AS$;" IS"
640 PRINT "PRODUCING";
650 INPUT U$
660 SUM=0
670 PRINT
680 PRINT "WHAT ARE THE ESTIMATED ";U$
690 PRINT "THAT ";AS$;" WILL"
700 PRINT "PRODUCE";
710 INPUT UN
720 DEP=(CAS-SAS)/UN
730 PRINT "USING THE UNITS OF"
740 PRINT "PRODUCTION METHOD THE"
750 PRINT "DEPRECIATION FOR"
770 PRINT AS$;" IS $";DEP
780 PRINT "PER UNIT"
790 FOR I=1 TO LAS
800 PRINT
810 PRINT "WHAT ARE THE EXPECTED"
820 PRINT U$;"FOR YEAR ";I;
830 INPUT UNP
840 TEMP=SUM
850 SUM=SUM+UNP
860 IF SUM<=UN THEN 900
870 UNP=UN-TEMP
880 IF UNP>0 THEN 900
890 UNP=0
900 ADE=DEP*UNP
910 ADE=INT((ADE+.005)*100)/100
920 PRINT
930 PRINT "THE ANNUAL DEPRECIATION"
940 PRINT "EXPENSE FOR YEAR ";I
950 PRINT "IS $";ADE
960 NEXT I
970 PRINT
980 PRINT "PRESS ENTER TO CONTINUE"
990 INPUT B$
1000 GO TO 1320
1010 DEP=2/LAS
1020 BAL=CAS
1030 FOR I=1 TO LAS
1040 ADE=DEP*BAL
1050 IF I=LAS THEN 1070
1060 IF (BAL-ADE)>SAS THEN 1080
1070 ADE=BAL-SAS
1080 BAL=BAL-ADE
1090 ADE=INT((ADE+.005)*100)/100
1100 PRINT "USING THE DECLINING BALANCE"
```

```
1110 PRINT "METHOD THE DEPRECIATION"
1120 PRINT "FOR YEAR ";I;" IS $";ADE
1130 PRINT
1140 PRINT "PRESS ENTER TO CONTINUE"
1150 INPUT B$
1160 NEXT I
1170 GO TO 1320
1180 SYD=LAS*((LAS+1)/2)
1190 TEMP=LAS
1200 FOR I=1 TO LAS
1210 DEP=TEMP/SYD*(CAS−SAS)
1220 DEP=INT((DEP+.005)*100)/100
1230 PRINT "USING THE SUM-OF-THE"
1240 PRINT "YEARS'-DIGITS METHOD"
1250 PRINT "THE ANNUAL DEPRECIATION"
1260 PRINT "FOR YEAR ";I;" IS $";DEP
1270 PRINT
1280 PRINT "PRESS ENTER TO CONTINUE"
1290 INPUT B$
1300 TEMP=TEMP−1
1310 NEXT I
1320 PRINT
1330 PRINT "DO YOU WISH TO RUN"
1340 PRINT "THE PROGRAM AGAIN"
1350 PRINT "(INPUT YES OR NO)";
1360 INPUT AN$
1370 IF AN$="YES" THEN 290
1380 END
```

Correlation and Regression Analysis
7

In the business world, analysts often examine the relationships between sets of data. Usually a change in one variable is examined to see how it effects a change in another. Analysts refer to the variable that can be changed as the independent variable, and to the variable that changes as the dependent variable. For example, suppose we were examining the effects of adjustments in an advertising budget on sales. In this case, the advertising budget is the independent variable, because it can be adjusted at will. The resulting sales amount is the dependent variable, because it depends on how much is spent on advertising.

ESTABLISHING CORRELATION COEFFICIENTS

Financial analysts are very interested in the relationship between dependent variables and independent variables. We can quantify the strength of this relationship with the correlation coefficient. The correlation coefficient tells us how strong the relationship between an independent and a dependent variable is.

By convention, correlation coefficients range from −1.0 to +1.0. If the correlation coefficient equals +1.0, we say the two variables are *perfectly positively correlated*. This means that an increase in the independent variable will always produce a proportional increase in the dependent variable. It also means that a decrease in the independent variable will always produce a proportional decrease in the dependent variable.

If the correlation coefficient equals −1.0, we say the variables are *perfectly negatively correlated*. This is analogous to the situation described above, except that in this case, a change in the independent variable will always produce a proportional change *in the opposite direction* in the dependent variable.

If the correlation coefficient equals zero, we know that there is absolutely no correlation between the two variables. This means that a change in one has no effect on the other. More importantly, it means that if a change in the supposedly dependent variable occurs when the independent variable is changed, the two events are unrelated.

In most real world situations, the correlation between two sets of data lies somewhere between −1.0 and 0, or 0 and +1.0. In this case, we have to examine how close the correlation coefficient is to either −1.0 or +1.0, and judge the degree of correlation. The closer the correlation coefficient is to either −1.0 or +1.0, the higher the correlation is.

A word of caution is in order, though. When examining two variables to determine if there is a relationship, a good measure of common sense is required. Suppose we were reviewing monthly data for the number of computer books sold and the number of people in the computer repair business. We would probably find a very high degree of correlation between the two variables, but we must recognize that one is not dependent on the other. Both are probably dependent on the same independent variable: the number of computers sold. Whenever we wish to test two variables for correlation, we must first determine if one could logically be expected to be dependent on the other.

USING REGRESSION TO PREDICT DEPENDENT VARIABLES

Now that we have established the concept of correlation, let's consider regression. Regression analysis may be used once we are satisfied that high correlation exists between an independent variable and a dependent variable. Regression analysis provides an equation that may be used to predict the dependent variable for a specified value of the independent variable. The regression equation is of the form

$$Y_r = A + B*X$$

Where Y_r is the dependent variable, A and B are constants, and X is the independent variable.

When we use regression analysis to predict values for the dependent variable there will be some measure of uncertainty involved. We can quantify this uncertainty by using a confidence interval. The confidence interval is expressed as a percent (typically 50, 68, 95, or 99 percent), and it defines confidence limits about the predicted value for the dependent variable. Suppose we specify a confidence interval of 95 percent. This means upper and lower confidence limits will be established for our predicted value of the dependent variable, such that we are 95 percent confident that the actual value will lie somewhere between these two limits.

Now that we understand the concepts associated with correlation and regression analysis, let's review a few examples to see how these concepts are used.

SAMPLE ANALYSIS: COMMISSIONS VS. SALES VOLUME

Adam Smith is a business consultant conducting a study for ten new car dealers. The dealers are interested in finding ways to motivate their respective sales forces to sell more new cars. Mr. Smith has decided to examine the relationship between the commission paid to the top salesperson at each dealership and the total sales for each salesperson during a one-month period. The sales commission, which is expressed as a percentage, is the independent variable. The sales volume is the dependent variable. Mr. Smith has assembled the data in Table 7.1.

To determine the relationship between the commission paid and the resulting sales volume, Mr. Smith wants to perform a correlation analysis. If he finds

TABLE 7.1
Comparison of Commissions and Sales

Salesperson	Percent Commission	Sales Volume
Tom Edwards	2	$ 28,000
Blake Putney	3	30,000
Ira Miller	7	145,000
Sue Epperson	1	29,000
Tony Jones	5	87,000
Frank Soo Hoo	6	85,000
Bill Edgar	3	22,000
Bob Fortunko	2	20,000
Bill Morane	1	19,000
Sally Hayes	4	45,000

high correlation between the two variables, he would like to use regression analysis to predict sales if the commission is 5 percent. Mr. Smith can use the Correlation and Regression Analysis program supplied on page 78.

Computer Request	Operator Input
WHAT IS THE NAME OF THE INDEPENDENT VARIABLE?	COMMISSION
WHAT IS THE NAME OF THE DEPENDENT VARIABLE?	SALES
HOW MANY SETS OF DATA ARE THERE?	10
ENTER EACH VALUE OF COMMISSION FOLLOWED BY A COMMA AND THEN THE CORRESPONDING VALUE OF SALES EACH TIME A QUESTION MARK APPEARS	
?	2,28000
?	3,30000
?	7,145000
?	1,29000
?	5,87000
?	6,85000
?	3,22000
?	2,20000
?	1,19000
?	4,45000

At this point, the screen will clear, and the computer will display the following information:

THE COEFFICIENT OF CORRELATION IS .91

THE LINEAR REGRESSION EQUATION IS

SALES = −11510.41667 + 18385.41667 * COMMISSION

DO YOU WANT TO USE THE
LINEAR REGRESSION EQUATION
TO CALCULATE
SALES
(INPUT YES OR NO)?

Since there is high correlation between sales and commission, let's use the regression equation to predict sales if we set the commission at 5 percent. Let's begin our analysis by examining the confidence limits at a confidence interval of 50 percent. Enter the input YES in response to the last question asked above, and here's what the computer will ask for:

Computer Request	Operator Input
WHAT IS THE VALUE OF COMMISSION?	5
WHAT CONFIDENCE INTERVAL WOULD YOU LIKE TO USE FOR UPPER AND LOWER CONFIDENCE LIMITS	
ENTER	
1 FOR 50 PERCENT	
2 FOR 68 PERCENT	
3 FOR 95 PERCENT	
4 FOR 99 PERCENT	
?	1

At this point, the screen will clear, and the computer will display the following information:

THE PREDICTED VALUE FOR
SALES IS
80416.67

WITH A LOWER
CONFIDENCE LIMIT OF
68282.69

AND AN UPPER
CONFIDENCE LIMIT OF
92550.64

PRESS ENTER TO CONTINUE
?

We can see from the above information that sales will equal $80,416.67 if we set the commission at 5 percent. The analysis also tells us we may be 50 percent confident the actual value of sales will lie somewhere between $68,282.69 and $92,550.64. Let's continue the analysis to see what the confidence limits will be if we use confidence intervals of 68, 95, and 99 percent. Press the ENTER key, and the program will continue as shown below:

Computer Request	Operator Input
DO YOU WANT TO USE THE LINEAR REGRESSION EQUATION TO CALCULATE SALES (INPUT YES OR NO)?	YES
WHAT IS THE VALUE OF COMMISSION?	5
WHAT CONFIDENCE INTERVAL WOULD YOU LIKE TO USE FOR UPPER AND LOWER CONFIDENCE LIMITS ENTER 1 FOR 50 PERCENT 2 FOR 68 PERCENT 3 FOR 95 PERCENT 4 FOR 99 PERCENT ?	2

After entering the above information, the screen will clear and the computer will display:

THE CALCULATED VALUE FOR
SALES IS
80416.67

WITH A LOWER
CONFIDENCE LIMIT OF
62306.26

AND AN UPPER
CONFIDENCE LIMIT OF
98527.08

PRESS ENTER TO CONTINUE
?

(press enter, and the program will continue with . . .)

Computer Request	Operator Input
DO YOU WANT TO USE THE LINEAR REGRESSION EQUATION TO CALCULATE SALES (INPUT YES OR NO)?	YES
WHAT IS THE VALUE OF COMMISSION?	5
WHAT CONFIDENCE INTERVAL WOULD YOU LIKE TO USE FOR UPPER AND LOWER CONFIDENCE LIMITS	
ENTER	
1 FOR 50 PERCENT	
2 FOR 68 PERCENT	
3 FOR 95 PERCENT	
4 FOR 99 PERCENT	
?	3

Once again, the screen will clear and the computer will show us the answer at the 95 percent confidence interval:

THE CALCULATED VALUE FOR
SALES IS
80416.67

WITH A LOWER
CONFIDENCE LIMIT OF
44920.26

AND AN UPPER
CONFIDENCE LIMIT OF
115913.07

PRESS ENTER TO CONTINUE
?

(press enter, and the program will continue with . . .)

Computer Request	Operator Input
DO YOU WANT TO USE THE LINEAR REGRESSION EQUATION TO CALCULATE SALES (INPUT YES OR NO)?	YES
WHAT IS THE VALUE OF COMMISSION?	5

Computer Request	Operator Input
WHAT CONFIDENCE INTERVAL WOULD YOU LIKE TO USE FOR UPPER AND LOWER CONFIDENCE LIMITS	
ENTER	

1 FOR 50 PERCENT
    2 FOR 68 PERCENT
    3 FOR 95 PERCENT
    4 FOR 99 PERCENT	

?	4

After entering the above information, the screen will clear, and the computer will show us the answer at the 99 percent confidence interval:

THE CALCULATED VALUE FOR
SALES IS
80416.67

WITH A LOWER
CONFIDENCE LIMIT OF
33691.81

AND AN UPPER
CONFIDENCE LIMIT OF
127141.53

PRESS ENTER TO CONTINUE
?

(press enter, and the program will continue with ...)

Computer Request	Operator Input
DO YOU WANT TO USE THE LINEAR REGRESSION EQUATION TO CALCULATE SALES (INPUT YES OR NO)?	NO
** DONE**	

Now that we've run the analysis for all four confidence levels, let's pause and examine the significance of our findings. We should note two things:

1. The predicted value for sales is the same for all four confidence levels ($80,416.67).
2. As the confidence interval increases, the span between the confidence limits also increases.

This is to be expected. The predicted value for sales should remain the same since, in all four cases, it is based on the same regression equation. The reason why the distance between the upper and lower confidence limits increases as we increase the confidence interval is somewhat more subtle. When we increase the confidence interval, we are demanding more confidence that the actual value will lie somewhere between the upper and lower confidence limits. To obtain this increased confidence, the limits must move further apart.

SAMPLE ANALYSIS: HOW PRICE AFFECTS VOLUME

Rita Thompson owns a restaurant. She is interested in determining the relationship between the price of a steak dinner and the number of meals sold, so that she will know how much steak to order if she raises the price to $13.75. She would like to establish a 50 percent confidence interval for her prediction. Ms. Thompson suspects that raising the price of a dinner will have an adverse effect on how many are sold, but she isn't sure. She reviewed her business records for the last two years to compile the data in Table 7.2.

Let's use the Correlation and Regression Analysis program to determine how price affects the number of steak dinners sold at Ms. Thompson's restaurant:

Computer Request	Operator Input
WHAT IS THE NAME OF THE INDEPENDENT VARIABLE?	PRICE
WHAT IS THE NAME OF THE DEPENDENT VARIABLE?	QUANTITY
HOW MANY SETS OF DATA ARE THERE?	8
ENTER EACH VALUE OF PRICE FOLLOWED BY A COMMA AND THEN THE CORRESPONDING VALUE OF QUANTITY EACH TIME A QUESTION MARK APPEARS	
?	7.99,562
?	8.50,525
?	8.50,530

Computer Request	Operator Input
?	11.99,433
?	10.99,488
?	11.99,437
?	10.50,512
?	13.00,392

At this point, the screen will clear, and the computer will provide the answer:

THE COEFFICIENT OF
CORRELATION IS −.96

THE LINEAR REGRESSION
EQUATION IS

QUANTITY = 792.6941964
+ −29.50579405 * PRICE

DO YOU WANT TO USE THE
LINEAR REGRESSION EQUATION
TO CALCULATE
QUANTITY
(INPUT YES OR NO)?

We can see that there is very high negative correlation between the price of a steak dinner and how many are sold (confirming Ms. Thompson's suspicion that raising the price will decrease the amount of meat she will have to order). Let's use the regression equation to predict the number of dinners that will be sold if the price is raised to $13.75, and establish the 50 percent confidence interval for our prediction. Enter the input YES, and the computer will continue as shown on the next page.

TABLE 7.2
Comparison of Price with Number of Meals Sold

Quarter	Price	No. Meals Sold
1-82	$ 7.99	562
2-82	8.50	525
3-82	8.50	530
4-82	11.99	433
1-83	10.99	488
2-83	11.99	437
3-83	10.50	512
4-83	13.00	392

Computer Request	Operator Input
WHAT IS THE VALUE OF PRICE?	13.75
WHAT CONFIDENCE INTERVAL WOULD YOU LIKE TO USE FOR UPPER AND LOWER CONFIDENCE LIMITS	
ENTER	
1 FOR 50 PERCENT	
2 FOR 68 PERCENT	
3 FOR 95 PERCENT	
4 FOR 99 PERCENT	
?	1

At this point, the screen will clear, and the computer will display the following information:

THE PREDICTED VALUE FOR
QUANTITY IS
386.99

WITH A LOWER
CONFIDENCE LIMIT OF
374.71

AND AN UPPER
CONFIDENCE LIMIT OF
399.27

PRESS ENTER TO CONTINUE
?

(press enter, and the program will continue with . . .)

Computer Request	Operator Input
DO YOU WANT TO USE THE LINEAR REGRESSION EQUATION TO CALCULATE QUANTITY (INPUT YES OR NO)?	NO
** DONE **	

You might wonder why Ms. Thompson would raise the price of a steak dinner, knowing that fewer meals will be sold. To answer this question, we'd like to suggest an interesting exercise. Calculate gross sales from the information presented at the beginning of this example (i.e., price times the number of meals sold), and then run the correlation and regression analysis for price and gross sales. You will find that, while there is high negative correlation between price and number of meals sold, there is also a fair degree of *positive* correlation between price and gross sales. In other words, while the number of meals sold will decrease if the price is raised to $13.75, the gross sales will increase.

We should recognize, though, that this doesn't mean Ms. Thompson can expect to keep increasing sales revenues simply by raising the price of the dinners she sells. Ultimately, she will begin to lose money if she keeps raising the price. This points to a caution that must be observed when using correlation and regression analysis. When the analysis is used to predict the dependent variable outside of the range of observed values, careful thought must be given to the prediction. We have to ask if we can logically expect the regression equation to remain true.

When setting up a correlation analysis, we also need to think about the likely dependencies that might exist between variables. Specifically, the effects of timing should be considered. Sometimes there may appear to be little or no correlation between variables. If we introduce a time lag into the analysis, though, we may be very surprised at the high degree of correlation that shows up. Let's take a look at another example to illustrate this point.

SAMPLE ANALYSIS: AD BUDGET VS. SALES VOLUME

The Cleburne Perfume Company wants to determine how effective its advertising is. The company wants to assess the impact on sales when the advertising budget is changed. Cleburne has the previous year's records to examine, compiled in Table 7.3.

TABLE 7.3
Comparison of Ad Budget and Sales

Month	Advertising Budget	Sales
Jan	$10,000	$1,580,391
Feb	15,000	1,300,782
Mar	12,000	1,793,482
Apr	18,000	1,484,386
May	10,000	2,128,364
Jun	12,000	1,173,488
Jul	18,000	1,284,357
Aug	15,000	2,122,399
Sep	18,000	1,683,122
Oct	15,000	2,344,789
Nov	18,000	1,486,392
Dec	10,000	2,438,686

Cleburne has decided to use its TI computer to run a correlation analysis:

Computer Request	Operator Input
WHAT IS THE NAME OF THE INDEPENDENT VARIABLE?	ADVERTISING
WHAT IS THE NAME OF THE DEPENDENT VARIABLE?	SALES
HOW MANY SETS OF DATA ARE THERE?	12
ENTER EACH VALUE OF ADVERTISING FOLLOWED BY A COMMA AND THEN THE CORRESPONDING VALUE OF SALES EACH TIME A QUESTION MARK APPEARS	
?	10000,1580391
?	15000,1300782
?	12000,1793482
?	18000,1484386
?	10000,2128364
?	12000,1173488
?	18000,1284357
?	15000,2122399
?	18000,1683122
?	15000,2344789
?	18000,1486392
?	10000,2438686

At this point, the screen will clear, and the computer will provide the answer:

THE COEFFICIENT OF CORRELATION IS −.39

THE LINEAR REGRESSION EQUATION IS

SALES = 2458669.391
+ −50.78008589 * ADVERTISING

DO YOU WANT TO USE THE LINEAR REGRESSION EQUATION TO CALCULATE SALES (INPUT YES OR NO)?	NO

** DONE **

Cleburne knows an answer like this shows little correlation between advertising and sales. The company is quite confused, until it realizes the advertising budget for one month may not have an effect until the next month. Cleburne has decided to run the analysis again, except this time it will examine the relationship between the monthly advertising budget and the next month's sales. In other words, the company wants to assess the effects of January's advertising budget on February's sales, and February's advertising budget on March's sales, and so on. Note that in this case, the company will only have 11 sets of data to assess, since one month is lost due to the effect of "lagging" the data. This time, Cleburne will use the data in Table 7.4.

The run for this data set is shown below.

Computer Request	Operator Input
WHAT IS THE NAME OF THE INDEPENDENT VARIABLE?	ADVERTISING
WHAT IS THE NAME OF THE DEPENDENT VARIABLE?	NEXT MONTH SALES
HOW MANY SETS OF DATA ARE THERE?	11
ENTER EACH VALUE OF ADVERTISING FOLLOWED BY A COMMA AND THEN THE CORRESPONDING VALUE OF NEXT MONTH SALES EACH TIME A QUESTION MARK APPEARS	
?	10000,1300782
?	15000,1793482
?	12000,1484386
?	18000,2128364
?	10000,1173488
?	12000,1284357

Computer Request	Operator Input
?	18000,2122399
?	15000,1683122
?	18000,2344789
?	15000,1486392
?	18000,2438686

At this point, the screen will clear, and the computer will provide the new answer:

THE COEFFICIENT OF
CORRELATION IS .94

THE LINEAR REGRESSION
EQUATION IS

NEXT MONTH SALES =
−166556.6197
+ 130.8842846 * ADVERTISING

DO YOU WANT TO USE THE
LINEAR REGRESSION EQUATION
TO CALCULATE
NEXT MONTH SALES
(INPUT YES OR NO)?   NO

** DONE **

Cleburne now knows that there is a high degree of positive correlation between the amount of money spent on advertising in a given month and the next month's sales. When advertising is increased, a fairly predictable increase can be expected in sales for the following month.

Table 7.4
Ad Budget Compared with Following Month's Sales

Advertising Budget	Next Month's Sales
$10,000	$1,300,782
15,000	1,793,482
12,000	1,484,386
18,000	2,128,364
10,000	1,173,488
12,000	1,284,357
18,000	2,122,399
15,000	1,683,122
18,000	2,344,789
15,000	1,486,392
18,000	2,438,686

FORMULAS

Formulas are included in the Program Listing; they are reviewed here for your reference.

COEFFICIENT OF CORRELATION

$$R = \frac{(N*TOTXY - TOTX*TOTY)}{\sqrt{(N*TOTX2 - TOTX*TOTX)*(N*TOTY2 - TOTY*TOTY)}}$$

(see program lines 460 to 490)

where

- R = coefficient of correlation
- N = number of observations
- $TOTXY$ = sum of the products of the values of the dependent and independent variables
- $TOTX$ = sum of the values of the independent variable
- $TOTY$ = sum of the values of the dependent variable
- $TOTX2$ = sum of the squares of the values of the independent variable
- $TOTY2$ = sum of the squares of the values of the dependent variable

LINEAR REGRESSION EQUATION

$$Y_r = A + B*X \quad \text{(see program lines 500–510 and 600–610)}$$

where

- Y_r = calculated value for the dependent variable
- A and B = constants
- X = specified value for the independent variable

STANDARD DEVIATION

$$S = \sqrt{(TOTY2 - A*TOTY - B*TOTXY)/(N - 2)}$$

(see program lines 500 to 520)

where

- S = standard deviation
- $TOTY2$ = sum of the squares of the values of the dependent variable

$TOTY$ = sum of the values of the dependent variable
$TOTXY$ = sum of the products of the values of the dependent and independent variables
A and B = constants
N = the number of observations

CONFIDENCE INTERVAL

$YCI = YC \pm TS$ (see program lines 1010 to 1020)

where

YCI = confidence interval for the calculated dependent variable
YC = calculated value of the dependent variable
TS = number of standard deviations

PROGRAM LISTING

CORRELATION AND REGRESSION ANALYSIS

```
100 CALL CLEAR
110 DIM X(100),Y(100)
120 PRINT "WHAT IS THE NAME"
130 PRINT "OF THE INDEPENDENT"
140 PRINT "VARIABLE";
150 INPUT FIRSV$
160 PRINT
170 PRINT "WHAT IS THE NAME"
180 PRINT "OF THE DEPENDENT"
190 PRINT "VARIABLE";
200 INPUT SECV$
210 PRINT
220 PRINT "HOW MANY SETS"
230 PRINT "OF DATA ARE THERE";
240 INPUT N
250 PRINT
260 PRINT
270 PRINT "ENTER EACH VALUE OF"
280 PRINT FIRSV$
290 PRINT "FOLLOWED BY A COMMA"
300 PRINT "AND THEN THE CORRESPONDING"
310 PRINT "VALUE OF"
320 PRINT SECV$
330 PRINT "EACH TIME A"
```

Note: If using the TI Professional Computer, substitute PRINT CHR$(12) for CALL CLEAR.

```
340 PRINT "QUESTION MARK APPEARS"
350 PRINT
360 FOR I=1 TO N
370 INPUT X(I),Y(I)
380 NEXT I
390 FOR I=1 TO N
400 TOTX=TOTX+X(I)
410 TOTY=TOTY+Y(I)
420 TOTX2=TOTX2+X(I)*X(I)
430 TOTY2=TOTY2+Y(I)*Y(I)
440 TOTXY=TOTXY+X(I)*Y(I)
450 NEXT I
460 MOMX=N*TOTX2−TOTX*TOTX
470 MOMY=N*TOTY2−TOTY*TOTY
480 MOMXY=N*TOTXY−TOTX*TOTY
490 R=MOMXY/SQR(MOMX*MOMY)
500 A=(TOTY*TOTX2−TOTX*TOTXY)/MOMX
510 B=MOMXY/MOMX
520 S=SQR((TOTY2−A*TOTY−B*TOTXY)/(N−2))
530 CALL CLEAR
540 PRINT "THE COEFFICIENT OF"
550 PRINT "CORRELATION IS ";INT((R+.005)*100)/100
560 PRINT
570 PRINT "THE LINEAR REGRESSION"
580 PRINT "EQUATION IS"
590 PRINT
600 PRINT SECV$;"=";A
610 PRINT "+";B;"*";FIRSV$
620 PRINT
630 PRINT "DO YOU WANT TO USE THE"
640 PRINT "LINEAR REGRESSION EQUATION"
650 PRINT "TO CALCULATE"
660 PRINT SECV$
670 PRINT "(INPUT YES OR NO)";
680 INPUT AN$
690 IF AN$="NO" THEN 1200
700 CALL CLEAR
710 PRINT "WHAT IS THE VALUE OF"
720 PRINT FIRSV$;
730 INPUT X1
740 PRINT
750 PRINT "WHAT CONFIDENCE INTERVAL"
760 PRINT "WOULD YOU LIKE TO USE FOR"
770 PRINT "UPPER AND LOWER"
780 PRINT "CONFIDENCE LIMITS"
790 PRINT
800 PRINT "ENTER"
```

```
810 PRINT
820 PRINT TAB(5);"1 FOR 50 PERCENT"
830 PRINT TAB(5);"2 FOR 68 PERCENT"
840 PRINT TAB(5);"3 FOR 95 PERCENT"
850 PRINT TAB(5);"4 FOR 99 PERCENT"
860 PRINT
870 INPUT CL
880 IF CL=1 THEN 930
890 IF CL=2 THEN 950
900 IF CL=3 THEN 970
910 IF CL=4 THEN 990
920 GO TO 750
930 TS=.67*S
940 GO TO 1000
950 TS=S
960 GO TO 1000
970 TS=1.96*S
980 GO TO 1000
990 TS=2.58*S
1000 YC=A+B*X1
1010 YCL=YC-TS
1020 YCU=YC+TS
1030 CALL CLEAR
1040 PRINT "THE PREDICTED VALUE FOR"
1050 PRINT SECV$;" IS"
1060 PRINT INT((YC+.005)*100)/100
1070 PRINT
1080 PRINT "WITH A LOWER"
1090 PRINT "CONFIDENCE LIMIT OF"
1100 PRINT INT((YCL+.005)*100)/100
1110 PRINT
1120 PRINT "AND AN UPPER"
1130 PRINT "CONFIDENCE LIMIT OF"
1140 PRINT INT((YCU+.005)*100)/100
1150 PRINT
1160 PRINT "PRESS ENTER TO CONTINUE"
1170 INPUT B$
1180 CALL CLEAR
1190 GO TO 630
1200 END
```

Multiple Linear Regression Analysis
8

In Chapter 7, Correlation and Regression Analysis, we examined the relationship between a dependent variable and a single independent variable. We'll take that approach further with the use of multiple linear regression analysis in this chapter. First, we'll develop a method for examining the relationship between a dependent variable and *several* independent variables. We'll use that information to develop an equation relating the dependent and independent variables, then use that equation to predict the dependent variable when changes are made to the independent variables. As in the last chapter, we'll also specify confidence intervals to give us a range for the resulting dependent variable.

Suppose we are interested in determining the relationship between sales (the dependent variable) and advertising, sales commission, and the price charged for the product (the independent variables). Multiple linear regression analysis allows us to use historical data to develop an equation that will define sales as a function of advertising, sales commissions, and price. We'll see how this is done in our example problem.

One word of caution is in order before we proceed. We must recognize that any equations developed using multiple linear regression analysis are based on past data. Using past information to predict the future will always involve a measure of uncertainty; therefore, we should always examine the environment to determine if anything has changed. Where change has occurred, we must then assess the probable effect on the relationships between the variables. If no effect is predicted, then we are on fairly safe ground, and we can use the multiple linear regression prediction.

SAMPLE ANALYSIS: ASSESSING THE EFFECTS OF SEVERAL VARIABLES ON SALES VOLUME

Wilson's Paint Company manufactures paint for commercial buildings. During the last six months the company has been experimenting with the advertising budget, the size of the sales commission, and the price charged for paint. It has recorded the data in Table 8.1.

Wilson would like to predict sales (at a 95-percent confidence interval) if the price charged for a gallon of paint is raised to $8.40, the sales commission lowered to 4 percent, and the advertising budget increased to $15,000.

Wilson knows from past experience that paint sales are not affected by the time of year; that is, the business is not seasonal. The economic environment has been fairly stable for the past 24 months and is expected to remain so for the forseeable future.

Let's use the multiple linear regression analysis program to make this prediction. Load the program into your TI-99/4A (the listing begins on page 86), enter the command RUN, and here's what the computer will ask for:

Computer Request	Operator Input
WHAT IS THE NAME OF THE DEPENDENT VARIABLE?	SALES
HOW MANY INDEPENDENT VARIABLES ARE RELATED TO SALES?	3
WHAT IS INDEPENDENT VARIABLE NUMBER 1?	ADVERTISING
WHAT IS INDEPENDENT VARIABLE NUMBER 2?	COMMISSION
WHAT IS INDEPENDENT VARIABLE NUMBER 3?	PRICE
HOW MANY SETS OF DATA ARE THERE?	6

Computer Request	Operator Input
DATA SET 1	
ADVERTISING?	12000
COMMISSION?	4
PRICE?	8.50
SALES?	149350
DATA SET 2	
ADVERTISING?	12000
COMMISSION?	3.5
PRICE?	8.30
SALES?	139000
DATA SET 3	
ADVERTISING?	13000
COMMISSION?	5
PRICE?	8.30
SALES?	165050
DATA SET 4	
ADVERTISING?	14000
COMMISSION?	4.5
PRICE?	8.25
SALES?	170400
DATA SET 5	
ADVERTISING?	13000
COMMISSION?	4.5
PRICE?	8.40
SALES?	168000
DATA SET 6	
ADVERTISING?	13500
COMMISSION?	5
PRICE?	8.35
SALES?	172000

TABLE 8.1
Comparing Sales with Ad Budget, Commission and Retail Price

Month	Sales	Advertising	Commission	Price
February	$149,350	$12,000	4%	$8.50
March	139,000	12,000	3.5%	8.30
April	165,050	13,000	5%	8.30
May	170,400	14,000	4.5%	8.25
June	168,000	13,000	4.5%	8.40
July	172,000	13,500	5%	8.35

At this point, the screen will clear and the computer will provide the multiple linear regression equation for the data we've entered:

BASED ON THE MULTIPLE
LINEAR REGRESSION
ANALYSIS THE EQUATION IS

SALES = −365494.82
+ 12.66 *ADVERTISING
+ 9052.85 *COMMISSION
+ 38632.12 *PRICE

The program will then ask if we want to use the multiple linear regression equation to estimate sales for a new set of variables. Since we do, we'll enter the input YES:

Computer Request	Operator Input
WOULD YOU LIKE TO ESTIMATE SALES FROM A SET OF INDEPENDENT VARIABLES (INPUT YES OR NO)?	YES
WHAT CONFIDENCE INTERVAL WOULD YOU LIKE TO USE FOR UPPER AND LOWER CONFIDENCE LIMITS ENTER 1 FOR 50 PERCENT 2 FOR 68 PERCENT 3 FOR 95 PERCENT 4 FOR 99 PERCENT ?	3
WHAT IS THE ADVERTISING FOR THE NEW DATA SET?	15000
WHAT IS THE COMMISSION FOR THE NEW DATA SET?	4
WHAT IS THE PRICE FOR THE NEW DATA SET?	8.40

At this point, the screen will clear, and the computer will provide the answer:

THE PREDICTED VALUE FOR
SALES IS
185126.39

```
WITH A LOWER
CONFIDENCE LIMIT OF
179168.01

AND AN UPPER
CONFIDENCE LIMIT OF
191084.76

PRESS ENTER TO CONTINUE
?
```

After you press enter, the computer will ask if you want to run the program for a new data set. Enter the input NO, and the program will terminate as shown:

```
WOULD YOU LIKE TO
ESTIMATE SALES
FROM A SET OF INDEPENDENT
VARIABLES
(INPUT YES OR NO)?                    NO
** DONE **
```

FORMULAS

The formulas are included in the Program Listing; they are reviewed here for easy reference.

THE MULTIPLE LINEAR REGRESSION EQUATION

$$Y_r = A + B*X_1 + C*X_2 + \ldots + K*X_{NI}$$ (see program lines 750-780, and 1230-1290)

where

Y_r = calculated value for the dependent variable
$A, B, C, \ldots K$ = constants
$X_1, X_2, \ldots X_{NI}$ = specified values for the independent variables
NI = number of independent variables

STANDARD DEVIATION

$$S = \sqrt{YRSUM/(N - NI - 1)}$$ (see program lines 800 to 870)

where

S = standard deviation
$YRSUM$ = sum of the squares of the differences between regression values and actual values for each observation
N = number of observations
NI = number of independent variables

CONFIDENCE INTERVAL

$$YCI = YC \pm TS \quad \text{(see program lines 1300-1310)}$$

where

YCI = confidence interval for calculated dependent variable
YC = calculated value of dependent variable
TS = number of standard deviations

PROGRAM LISTING

MULTIPLE LINEAR REGRESSION ANALYSIS

```
100 CALL CLEAR
110 DIM TEMP(25),MA(25,25),DV$(25),
YRT(25),YR(25,10),YR1(25)
120 PRINT "WHAT IS THE NAME"
130 PRINT "OF THE DEPENDENT"
140 PRINT "VARIABLE";
150 INPUT DE$
160 PRINT
170 PRINT "HOW MANY INDEPENDENT"
180 PRINT "VARIABLES ARE RELATED"
190 PRINT "TO ";DE$;
200 INPUT NI
210 HOLD1=NI+1
220 HOLD2=NI+2
230 TEMP(1)=1
240 FOR KK=1 TO NI
250 PRINT
260 PRINT "WHAT IS INDEPENDENT"
270 PRINT "VARIABLE"
280 PRINT "NUMBER";KK;
```

Note: If using the TI Professional Computer, substitute PRINT CHR$(12) for CALL CLEAR.

```
290 INPUT DV$(KK)
300 NEXT KK
310 PRINT
320 PRINT "HOW MANY SETS OF"
330 PRINT "DATA ARE THERE";
340 INPUT N
350 FOR C1=1 TO N
360 PRINT
370 PRINT "DATA SET ";C1
380 FOR C2=1 TO NI
390 HOLD3=C2+1
400 PRINT DV$(C2);
410 INPUT TEMP(HOLD3)
420 YR(C1,HOLD3)=TEMP(HOLD3)
430 NEXT C2
440 PRINT DE$;
450 INPUT TEMP(HOLD2)
460 YR1(C1)=TEMP(HOLD2)
470 FOR C3=1 TO HOLD1
480 FOR C4=1 TO HOLD2
490 MA(C3,C4)=TEMP(C4)*TEMP(C3)+MA(C3,C4)
500 NEXT C4
510 NEXT C3
520 NEXT C1
530 FOR C1=1 TO HOLD1
540 TP1=MA(C1,C1)
550 FOR C3=1 TO HOLD2
560 MA(C1,C3)=MA(C1,C3)/TP1
570 NEXT C3
580 FOR C2=1 TO HOLD1
590 IF C2=C1 THEN 640
600 TP1=MA(C2,C1)
610 FOR C3=1 TO HOLD2
620 MA(C2,C3)=MA(C2,C3)-MA(C1,C3)*TP1
630 NEXT C3
640 NEXT C2
650 NEXT C1
660 FOR JJ=1 TO HOLD1
670 MA(JJ,HOLD2)=INT((MA(JJ,HOLD2)+.005)*100)/100
680 NEXT JJ
690 CALL CLEAR
700 PRINT "BASED ON THE MULTIPLE"
710 PRINT "LINEAR REGRESSION"
720 PRINT "ANALYSIS THE EQUATION IS"
730 PRINT
740 PRINT
750 PRINT DE$;" = ";MA(1,HOLD2)
```

```
760 FOR C1=2 TO HOLD1
770 PRINT "+";MA(C1,HOLD2);"*";DV$(C1-1)
780 NEXT C1
790 PRINT
800 FOR C1=1 TO N
810 FOR C2=2 TO HOLD1
820 YRT(C1)=YRT(C1)+MA(C2,HOLD2)*YR(C1,C2)
830 NEXT C2
840 YRT(C1)=YRT(C1)+MA(1,HOLD2)
850 YRSUM=(YR1(C1)-YRT(C1))∧2+YRSUM
860 NEXT C1
870 S=SQR(YRSUM/(N-NI-1))
880 SOL=MA(1,HOLD2)
890 PRINT
900 PRINT "WOULD YOU LIKE TO"
910 PRINT "ESTIMATE ";DE$
920 PRINT "FROM A SET OF INDEPENDENT"
930 PRINT "VARIABLES"
940 PRINT "(INPUT YES OR NO)";
950 INPUT AN$
960 IF AN$="NO" THEN 1490
970 PRINT
980 PRINT "WHAT CONFIDENCE INTERVAL"
990 PRINT "WOULD YOU LIKE TO USE FOR"
1000 PRINT "UPPER AND LOWER"
1010 PRINT "CONFIDENCE LIMITS"
1020 PRINT
1030 PRINT "ENTER"
1040 PRINT
1050 PRINT TAB(5);"1 FOR 50 PERCENT"
1060 PRINT TAB(5);"2 FOR 68 PERCENT"
1070 PRINT TAB(5);"3 FOR 95 PERCENT"
1080 PRINT TAB(5);"4 FOR 99 PERCENT"
1090 PRINT
1100 INPUT CL
1110 IF CL=1 THEN 1160
1120 IF CL=2 THEN 1180
1130 IF CL=3 THEN 1200
1140 IF CL=4 THEN 1220
1150 GO TO 980
1160 TS=.67*S
1170 GO TO 1230
1180 TS=S
1190 GO TO 1230
1200 TS=1.96*S
1210 GO TO 1230
1220 TS=2.58*S
```

```
1230 FOR C2=1 TO NI
1240 PRINT
1250 PRINT "WHAT IS THE ";DV$(C2)
1260 PRINT "FOR THE NEW DATA SET";
1270 INPUT ZZ
1280 SOL=SOL+MA(C2+1,HOLD2)*ZZ
1290 NEXT C2
1300 YCL=SOL-TS
1310 YCU=SOL+TS
1320 CALL CLEAR
1330 PRINT "THE PREDICTED VALUE FOR"
1340 PRINT DE$;" IS"
1350 PRINT INT((SOL+.005)*100)/100
1360 PRINT
1370 PRINT "WITH A LOWER"
1380 PRINT "CONFIDENCE LIMIT OF"
1390 PRINT INT((YCL+.005)*100)/100
1400 PRINT
1410 PRINT "AND AN UPPER"
1420 PRINT "CONFIDENCE LIMIT OF"
1430 PRINT INT((YCU+.005)*100)/100
1440 PRINT
1450 PRINT "PRESS ENTER TO CONTINUE"
1460 INPUT B$
1470 CALL CLEAR
1480 GO TO 880
1490 END
```

Inventory Level Analysis
9

Inventories are an important part of any company's assets. They represent the ability to quickly respond to customer demands. If inventories become too large, the company will suffer, since it will have money tied up that could be better used elsewhere. Similarly, if inventories are too small, the company will again suffer because it will not be able to respond readily to demands for its products, and customers may go elsewhere.

ESTABLISHING EOQ AND SAFETY STOCK

Determining the proper inventory level (i.e., neither too high nor too low) is therefore an important consideration for any business. One of the most common methods used to make this determination involves a two-step procedure:

1. First, the optimal ordering quantity and optimal average inventory level are defined through the use of economic ordering quantity analysis. This analytical technique allows a company to determine how much inventory it should order and maintain in an idealized situation (i.e., delivery times and demand remain constant). Under these idealized conditions, economic ordering quantity analysis defines the ordering quantity and inventory level necessary to minimize inventory ordering and carrying costs while providing sufficient inventory to meet customer demands.

2. Next, a safety stock is defined. The safety stock considers that both demand and delivery times will vary, and is added to the inventory level to prevent the company from experiencing stockouts.

Before looking at the example we've included to illustrate inventory level analysis, we need to understand several other concepts. The first of these is inventory carrying costs, or costs incurred as a result of keeping inventories on hand. These costs typically include such things as storage, handling, obsolescence, and insurance. For most businesses, annual inventory carrying costs are approximately 25 percent of the value of the inventory.

We also need to understand the concepts of fixed and variable costs for placing an order. Fixed costs are those incurred whenever an order is placed, regardless of the quantity ordered. Fixed costs include such things as long-distance telephone calls, clerical time required for processing the order, setting up production equipment, and other costs that are peculiar to the type of business involved. Variable costs are those associated with ordering each item and will vary as the quantity ordered varies. A portion of the shipping and receiving costs will fall into this category (i.e., they will be dependent on the number of units ordered). Other types of variable costs may also be incurred, depending on the nature of the business. Note that variable costs do not include the price of the item. Variable costs are only those costs that come about because of the ordering process.

Another concept we need to understand is that of the purchase price of the items being ordered. The price we are interested in is the price that the ordering business uses for valuing its inventory. For the purposes of inventory level analysis, we are not interested in the ultimate sales price of the item.

Next, we have to understand what is meant by the optimal average inventory, as opposed to the economic ordering quantity. The economic ordering quantity is the optimal quantity to order, such that the sum of carrying costs and ordering costs is minimized while maintaining an inventory adequate to the needs of the business. The optimal average inventory is the average amount of inventory that will be on hand as a result of ordering the economic ordering quantity. As we have mentioned, economic ordering quantity and optimal average inventory are concepts associated with an idealized situation. In the real world, demand is often uneven and delivery times vary.

Safety stocks are used to address this problem. A safety stock is an addition to the inventory level defined in our idealized situation, and it is designed to prevent a stockout. Generally, the safety stock will be determined by four things:

1. Variations in demand rate
2. Variations in delivery schedule
3. Costs of ordering and carrying additional inventory
4. Cost of lost sales due to a stockout

The inventory level analysis program included in this chapter will assess variations in the demand rate and delivery schedule at specified confidence levels. The program will then recommend an appropriate safety stock, and show the probability of a stockout along with the cost of carrying the recommended safety stock. The cost of carrying the recommended safety stock will have to be balanced against the cost of a stockout by the person using the program. Since these costs involve many intangibles (damage to the reputation of the business, forcing customers to turn to competitors with subsequent loss of repeat business, etc.), we do not attempt to quantify this cost in the inventory level analysis program. When using the program you will have to compare the specified costs of carrying additional inventory and the probabilities of a stockout against what you believe the cost of lost sales will be.

SAMPLE ANALYSIS: DETERMINING OPTIMAL INVENTORY

Benedetto's Tire and Wheel Center sells 10,000 tires per year. The business has to pay $34.67 for each tire. The fixed cost per order is $300, which is the cost incurred as a result of processing the order. The variable cost of ordering each tire is $1.22, which is the cost incurred due to shipping. Based on past experience, the carrying cost is known to be 25 percent of the inventory value. Mr. Benedetto, the proprietor, knows that both demand and delivery times are uneven. He has assembled the following information:

Order Number	Delivery Time (weeks)
1	1.2
2	1.0
3	0.8
4	1.0
5	0.8
6	0.8

Week	Demand
1	190
2	186
3	200
4	210
5	204
6	192
7	225
8	188
9	192
10	190

Based on the above information, Mr. Benedetto would like to determine the economic ordering quantity and the optimal average inventory. He would also like to know the required safety stock (using a 50 percent confidence interval for estimates of demand and delivery times), and the total annual cost to order and carry the inventory with the safety stock. Mr. Benedetto would then like to know the probability of a stockout if he carries the recommended safety stock, as well as the annual carrying cost incurred by the safety stock alone.

We can find the answers to these questions with the Inventory Level Analysis program. Load the program into your TI-99/4A (the listing begins on page 98), enter the command RUN, and here's what the computer will ask for:

Computer Request	Operator Input
WHAT ARE THE EXPECTED SALES (EXPRESSED IN UNITS) PER YEAR?	10000
WHAT IS THE FIXED COST OF PLACING AND RECEIVING AN ORDER?	300
WHAT IS THE VARIABLE COST OF PLACING AN ORDER?	1.22
WHAT IS THE PRICE PER UNIT?	34.67
WHAT IS THE CARRYING COST (EXPRESSED AS A PERCENT) OF INVENTORY VALUE?	25
HOW MANY DATA POINTS DO YOU HAVE FOR DELIVERY TIME?	6
INPUT EACH DELIVERY TIME (EXPRESSED IN WEEKS) EACH TIME A QUESTION MARK APPEARS	
?	1.2
?	1.0
?	0.8
?	1.0
?	0.8
?	0.8
HOW MANY DATA POINTS DO YOU HAVE FOR DEMAND RATE?	10

Computer Request	Operator Input
INPUT EACH DEMAND RATE (ON A WEEKLY BASIS) EACH TIME A QUESTION MARK APPEARS	
?	190
?	186
?	200
?	210
?	204
?	192
?	225
?	188
?	192
?	190

SELECT A CONFIDENCE INTERVAL
FOR DELIVERY TIME
AND DEMAND RATE

ENTER

    1 FOR 50 PERCENT
    2 FOR 68 PERCENT
    3 FOR 95 PERCENT
    4 FOR 99 PERCENT

?   1

At this point, the screen will clear, and the computer will display the following information:

THE OPTIMAL QUANTITY
TO ORDER IS 832

THE OPTIMAL AVERAGE
INVENTORY (DISREGARDING
SAFETY STOCK) IS 416

PRESS ENTER TO CONTINUE
?

       (press enter, and the program will continue with ...)

THE RECOMMENDED
SAFETY STOCK
(CONSIDERING THE
DISTRIBUTIONS OF
DELIVERY TIME AND
WEEKLY DEMAND)
IS 56

```
THE AVERAGE INVENTORY
(WITH SAFETY STOCK)
IS 472

WITH THIS SAFETY STOCK
THE PROBABILITY OF A
STOCKOUT DOES NOT EXCEED
6.25 PERCENT

PRESS ENTER TO CONTINUE
?
```

(press enter, and the program will continue with . . .)

```
THE TOTAL ANNUAL COST OF
ORDERING AND CARRYING
INVENTORIES (INCLUDING
THE SAFETY STOCK)
IS $19896.83

THE ANNUAL CARRYING COST
FOR THE SAFETY STOCK
ALONE IS $485.38

** DONE **
```

This means that to minimize ordering costs, Benedetto's Tire and Wheel Center should order 832 tires each time it places an order (assuming the business has a safety stock of 56 tires on hand when the order arrives). If they keep a safety stock of 56 tires, this will result in the business maintaining an average inventory of 472 tires. As the answer shows, the annual cost of maintaining this inventory will be $19,896.83, which is the lowest cost Benedetto's can incur if they wish to maintain an inventory adequate to meet the needs of the business. With the recommended safety stock of 56 tires, the probability of a stockout does not exceed 6.25 percent. The annual cost of carrying the 56-tire safety stock is $485.38. Mr. Benedetto has to decide if this annual carrying cost is less than what his business would likely suffer if a stockout occurred.

FORMULAS

The formulas are all included in the Program Listing; they are reviewed here for easy reference.

ECONOMIC ORDERING QUANTITY

$$EQ = \sqrt{2*F*S/(C*P)} \quad \text{(see program line 360)}$$

where

EQ = economic ordering quantity
F = fixed cost of placing and receiving an order
S = expected sales per year
C = inventory carrying cost
P = price per unit

AVERAGE INVENTORY

$$AE = EQ/2 \quad \text{(see program line 380)}$$

where

AE = average inventory level
EQ = economic ordering quantity

AVERAGE DELIVERY TIME

$$DTM = DTOT/NT \quad \text{(see program line 550)}$$

where

DTM = average delivery time
$DTOT$ = sum of delivery times
NT = number of observations for delivery time

STANDARD DEVIATION OF DELIVERY TIME

$$SDEL = \sqrt{(DTOT2 - NT*DTM*DTM)/(NT - 1)}$$
(see program line 560)

where

$SDEL$ = standard deviation of the delivery time
$DTOT2$ = sum of the squares of observed delivery times
NT = number of observations
DTM = average delivery time

AVERAGE DEMAND RATE

$$DRM = S/52 \quad \text{(see program line 730)}$$

where

DRM = average weekly demand rate
S = anticipated annual sales

STANDARD DEVIATION OF DEMAND RATE

$$SDEM = \sqrt{(DRTOT2 - ND*DRM*DRM)/(ND - 1)}$$
(see program line 740)

where

$SDEM$ = standard deviation of demand rate
$DRTOT2$ = sum of the squares of observed weekly demand rates
ND = number of observations
DRM = average weekly demand rate

SAFETY STOCK

$$SS = (DTM + SDEL)*(DRM + SDEM) - DTM*DRM$$
(see program line 1060)

where

SS = safety stock
DTM = average delivery time
$SDEL$ = standard deviation of the delivery time
DRM = average weekly demand rate
$SDEM$ = standard deviation of the demand rate

TOTAL ANNUAL CARRYING COST

$$T = C*P*(EQ/2 + SS) + F*S/EQ + V*S$$
(see program line 1080)

where

T = total annual carrying cost
C = inventory carrying cost
P = price per unit
EQ = economic ordering quantity
SS = safety stock

F = fixed cost of placing and receiving an order
S = annual sales
V = variable cost of placing and receiving an order

ANNUAL CARRYING COST OF SAFETY STOCK

$$T1 = C*P*SS \quad \text{(see program line 1100)}$$

where

$T1$ = annual carrying cost of safety stock
C = inventory carrying cost
P = price per unit
SS = safety stock

PROGRAM LISTING

INVENTORY LEVEL ANALYSIS

```
100 CALL CLEAR
110 DIM DT(100),DR(100)
120 PRINT "WHAT ARE THE EXPECTED"
130 PRINT "SALES (EXPRESSED IN UNITS)"
140 PRINT "PER YEAR";
150 INPUT S
160 PRINT
170 PRINT "WHAT IS THE FIXED COST"
180 PRINT "OF PLACING AND RECEIVING"
190 PRINT "AN ORDER";
200 INPUT F
210 PRINT
220 PRINT "WHAT IS THE VARIABLE"
230 PRINT "COST OF PLACING"
240 PRINT "AN ORDER";
250 INPUT V
260 PRINT
270 PRINT "WHAT IS THE PRICE"
280 PRINT "PER UNIT";
290 INPUT P
300 PRINT
310 PRINT "WHAT IS THE CARRYING COST"
320 PRINT "(EXPRESSED AS A PERCENT)"
```

Note: If using the TI Professional Computer, substitute PRINT CHR$(12) for CALL CLEAR.

```
330 PRINT "OF INVENTORY VALUE";
340 INPUT C
350 C=C/100
360 EQ=SQR(2*F*S/(C*P))
370 EQ=INT(EQ+.5)
380 AE=EQ/2
390 CALL CLEAR
400 PRINT "HOW MANY DATA POINTS"
410 PRINT "DO YOU HAVE FOR"
420 PRINT "DELIVERY TIME";
430 INPUT NT
440 PRINT
450 PRINT "INPUT EACH DELIVERY TIME"
460 PRINT "(EXPRESSED IN WEEKS)"
470 PRINT "EACH TIME A"
480 PRINT "QUESTION MARK APPEARS"
490 PRINT
500 FOR I=1 TO NT
510 INPUT DT(I)
520 DTOT=DTOT+DT(I)
530 DTOT2=DTOT2+DT(I)*DT(I)
540 NEXT I
550 DTM=DTOT/NT
560 SDEL=SQR((DTOT2−NT*DTM*DTM)/(NT−1))
570 CALL CLEAR
580 PRINT "HOW MANY DATA POINTS"
590 PRINT "DO YOU HAVE FOR"
600 PRINT "DEMAND RATE";
610 INPUT ND
620 PRINT
630 PRINT "INPUT EACH DEMAND RATE"
640 PRINT "(ON A WEEKLY BASIS)"
650 PRINT "EACH TIME A"
660 PRINT "QUESTION MARK APPEARS"
670 PRINT
680 FOR I=1 TO ND
690 INPUT DR(I)
700 DRTOT=DRTOT+DR(I)
710 DRTOT2=DRTOT2+DR(I)*DR(I)
720 NEXT I
730 DRM=S/52
740 SDEM=SQR((DRTOT2−ND*DRM*DRM)/(ND−1))
750 CALL CLEAR
760 PRINT "SELECT A CONFIDENCE INTERVAL"
770 PRINT "FOR DELIVERY TIME"
780 PRINT "AND DEMAND RATE"
790 PRINT
```

```
800 PRINT "ENTER"
810 PRINT
820 PRINT TAB(5);"1 FOR 50 PERCENT"
830 PRINT TAB(5);"2 FOR 68 PERCENT"
840 PRINT TAB(5);"3 FOR 95 PERCENT"
850 PRINT TAB(5);"4 FOR 99 PERCENT"
860 PRINT
870 INPUT CL
880 IF CL=1 THEN 930
890 IF CL=2 THEN 1050
900 IF CL=3 THEN 970
910 IF CL=4 THEN 1010
920 GO TO 750
930 SDEL=.67*SDEL
940 SDEM=.67*SDEM
950 PRSO=6.25
960 GO TO 1060
970 SDEL=1.96*SDEL
980 SDEM=1.96*SDEM
990 PRSO=.0625
1000 GO TO 1060
1010 SDEL=2.58*SDEL
1020 SDEM=2.58*SDEM
1030 PRSO=.0025
1040 GO TO 1060
1050 PRSO=2.56
1060 SS=(DTM+SDEL)*(DRM+SDEM)−DTM*DRM
1070 SS=INT(SS+.5)
1080 T=C*P*(EQ/2+SS)+F*S/EQ+V*S
1090 T=INT((T+.005)*100)/100
1100 T1=C*P*SS
1110 CALL CLEAR
1120 PRINT "THE OPTIMAL QUANTITY"
1130 PRINT "TO ORDER IS";
1140 PRINT EQ
1150 PRINT
1160 PRINT "THE OPTIMAL AVERAGE"
1170 PRINT "INVENTORY (DISREGARDING"
1180 PRINT "SAFETY STOCK) IS";AE
1190 PRINT
1200 PRINT "PRESS ENTER TO CONTINUE"
1210 INPUT A$
1220 CALL CLEAR
1230 PRINT "THE RECOMMENDED"
1240 PRINT "SAFETY STOCK"
1250 PRINT "(CONSIDERING THE"
1260 PRINT "DISTRIBUTIONS OF"
```

```
1270 PRINT "DELIVERY TIME AND"
1280 PRINT "WEEKLY DEMAND)"
1290 PRINT "IS";SS
1300 PRINT
1310 PRINT "THE AVERAGE INVENTORY"
1320 PRINT "(WITH SAFETY STOCK)"
1330 PRINT "IS";AE+SS
1340 PRINT
1350 PRINT "WITH THIS SAFETY STOCK"
1360 PRINT "THE PROBABILITY OF A"
1370 PRINT "STOCKOUT DOES NOT EXCEED"
1380 PRINT PRSO;" PERCENT"
1390 PRINT
1400 PRINT "PRESS ENTER TO CONTINUE"
1410 INPUT A$
1420 CALL CLEAR
1430 PRINT "THE TOTAL ANNUAL COST OF"
1440 PRINT "ORDERING AND CARRYING"
1450 PRINT "INVENTORIES (INCLUDING"
1460 PRINT "THE SAFETY STOCK)"
1470 PRINT "IS $";T
1480 PRINT
1490 PRINT "THE ANNUAL CARRYING COST"
1500 PRINT "FOR THE SAFETY STOCK"
1510 PRINT "ALONE IS $";T1
1520 END
```

Portfolio Analysis
10

Portfolio analysis is used to evaluate a collection of stocks. Let's begin our discussion by describing the terms used in portfolio analysis.

PORTFOLIO: a collection of stocks in a single account.

RISK: the probability of an increase or a decrease in the value of a stock, or a portfolio of stocks.

BETA: a measure of how a stock, or a portfolio of stocks, reacts to overall market performance. Beta coefficients are used to quantify the expected magnitude and direction of this reaction.

EXPECTED RATE OF RETURN: the expected change in the value of a particular stock, or a portfolio of stocks. Expected rate of return takes into account both capital appreciation and stock dividends.

RISK-FREE RATE OF RETURN: as the name implies, this is the rate of return that can be realized if no risk is involved. Generally, this is the rate of return provided by U.S. Treasury securities.

EXPECTED MARKET RATE OF RETURN: the return on the portfolio of all stocks in the market (i.e., the average return of all stocks).

UNDERSTANDING BETA COEFFICIENTS

With these definitions in mind, let's talk a little bit more about beta and beta coefficients before we look at our sample applications. Beta coefficients are used to quantify the reaction of a stock to overall market performance. Beta coefficients are based on the concept that the market, as a whole, has a beta of 1.0. Therefore, if a stock has a beta exactly equal to 1.0, it will behave exactly as the market does. If the market goes up 10 percent, the price of the stock will go up 10 percent; if the market goes down 10 percent, the price of the stock will go down 10 percent.

If the stock has a beta greater than 1.0, it will generally move in the same direction the market does, but by a greater amount. When the market goes up, a stock with a beta greater than 1.0 will go up an even greater amount; when the market goes down, such a stock will show a correspondingly greater loss.

If the stock has a beta less than 1.0 (but greater than 0), it will go up when the market does, but by a smaller amount. Similarly, the stock will go down when the overall market declines, but by a smaller amount.

Generally speaking, betas significantly greater than 1.0 are associated with riskier stocks. This makes sense, because high risk stocks generally overreact to any trends shown in the market. New issues associated with highly leveraged companies fall into this category. Larger, more established companies have betas that are more nearly equal to 1.0. These companies tend to react as the market does.

Some companies' stocks have negative betas. The stocks of these companies generally react in a manner opposite to that of the overall market. If the market declines, the value of these stocks increases, and vice versa. Such companies are called countercyclical. Gold mines are a good example. When the stock market as a whole is falling, gold becomes more valuable, and the price of gold mine stock goes up. To some extent, the stock of beer companies behaves similarly. During depressed economic conditions, people tend to drink more beer (and to switch to beer from more expensive drinks), which causes the stock of beer companies to go up.

Beta coefficients for individual stocks are found in most stock indices and guides. They can also be obtained by calling any stock brokerage house.

When several stocks are combined in a portfolio, the investor who owns the portfolio will want to have some way of gauging the riskiness of the entire portfolio. Each stock in the portfolio will have a different beta. Some will go up more than the market does, some will go up less, some will behave about as the market does, and some will move in the opposite direction. Just as a beta is assigned for the individual stocks in the portfolio, a beta for the entire portfolio can be developed. The new beta for the portfolio will provide an indication as to how much the value of the entire portfolio will change, and in what direction, with changes in the overall market.

The expected return of the portfolio can be developed once the beta for the portfolio is known, and as we'll see in a few moments, our program will provide both. One thing that needs to be kept in mind, though, is that as the beta of the portfolio increases, so will the expected return on the portfolio. That doesn't mean higher returns will automatically occur with higher betas. If that were the case, we'd simply build a portfolio of the riskiest stocks we could find, and wait for huge returns. The association of high betas with high expected rates of return should be interpreted to mean that the potential reward must be greater (or the expected rate of return should increase) as the riskiness of the portfolio increases. A large risk should be justified by a large potential reward.

SAMPLE ANALYSIS: REDUCING THE RISK

Stan Singer has a portfolio of fairly risky stocks. He'd like to reduce the riskiness of his portfolio by selling some of the high risk stocks and replacing them with stocks of lower risk.

Mr. Singer's current portfolio consists of the 12 stocks delineated in Table 10.1.

Mr. Singer wants to sell Nuclear Medicine, Solar Energy, Hi-Tek Industries, and Lunar Radiographics. He wants to take the money from the sale of these stocks and buy as much stock in General American industries as he can. General American has a beta of 1.05, and currently sells for $62.00 per share. The risk-free rate of return (or the rate of return on U.S. Government treasury bills) is 10.9 percent. The market rate of return (or the return on an average stock) is 14.2 percent.

TABLE 10.1
Singer's Portfolio

Stock	Quantity	Price	Beta
Advance Technology	500	$22.00	1.45
Solar Energy	350	18.75	1.80
Nuclear Medicine	500	32.00	1.75
Offshore Explorations	100	25.25	1.50
Hi-Tek Industries	400	13.75	1.85
Lunar Radiographics	350	15.00	1.70
Aluminum Recyclers	100	47.00	1.50
Oil Services	500	19.25	1.30
Tahoe Concepts	300	11.00	1.40
Nicholson Financial	500	22.50	1.25
Global Explorations	200	39.00	1.20
American Federated	500	42.00	1.35

What is total value, beta, and expected rate of return for Mr. Singer's present portfolio? What will they be when he sells the four stocks listed above and replaces them with General American stock?

Let's use the Portfolio Analysis program to answer these questions. Load the program (the listing begins on page 112), enter the command RUN, and here's what the computer will ask for:

Computer Request	Operator Input
HOW MANY STOCKS ARE IN THE PORTFOLIO?	12
WHAT IS THE NAME OF STOCK 1?	ADVANCE TECHNOLOGY
WHAT IS THE PRICE OF ADVANCE TECHNOLOGY?	22.00
HOW MANY SHARES OF ADVANCE TECHNOLOGY ARE IN THE PORTFOLIO?	500
WHAT IS THE BETA FOR ADVANCE TECHNOLOGY?	1.45
WHAT IS THE NAME OF STOCK 2?	SOLAR ENERGY
WHAT IS THE PRICE OF SOLAR ENERGY?	18.75
HOW MANY SHARES OF SOLAR ENERGY ARE IN THE PORTFOLIO?	350
WHAT IS THE BETA FOR SOLAR ENERGY?	1.80
WHAT IS THE NAME OF STOCK 3?	NUCLEAR MEDICINE
WHAT IS THE PRICE OF NUCLEAR MEDICINE?	32.00
HOW MANY SHARES OF NUCLEAR MEDICINE ARE IN THE PORTFOLIO?	500
WHAT IS THE BETA FOR NUCLEAR MEDICINE?	1.75
WHAT IS THE NAME OF STOCK 4?	OFFSHORE EXPLORATIONS
WHAT IS THE PRICE OF OFFSHORE EXPLORATIONS?	25.25

Computer Request	Operator Input
HOW MANY SHARES OF OFFSHORE EXPLORATIONS ARE IN THE PORTFOLIO?	100
WHAT IS THE BETA FOR OFFSHORE EXPLORATIONS?	1.50
WHAT IS THE NAME OF STOCK 5?	HI-TEK INDUSTRIES
WHAT IS THE PRICE OF HI-TEK INDUSTRIES?	13.75
HOW MANY SHARE OF HI-TEK INDUSTRIES ARE IN THE PORTFOLIO?	400
WHAT IS THE BETA FOR HI-TEK INDUSTRIES?	1.85
WHAT IS THE NAME OF STOCK 6?	LUNAR RADIOGRAPHICS
WHAT IS THE PRICE OF LUNAR RADIOGRAPHICS?	15.00
HOW MANY SHARES OF LUNAR RADIOGRAPHICS ARE IN THE PORTFOLIO?	350
WHAT IS THE BETA FOR LUNAR RADIOGRAPHICS?	1.70
WHAT IS THE NAME OF STOCK 7?	ALUMINUM RECYCLERS
WHAT IS THE PRICE OF ALUMINUM RECYCLERS?	47.00
HOW MANY SHARES OF ALUMINUM RECYCLERS ARE IN THE PORTFOLIO?	100
WHAT IS THE BETA FOR ALUMINUM RECYCLERS?	1.50
WHAT IS THE NAME OF STOCK 8?	OIL SERVICES
WHAT IS THE PRICE OF OIL SERVICES?	19.25
HOW MANY SHARES OF OIL SERVICES ARE IN THE PORTFOLIO?	500
WHAT IS THE BETA FOR OIL SERVICES?	1.30

Computer Request	Operator Input
WHAT IS THE NAME OF STOCK 9?	TAHOE CONCEPTS
WHAT IS THE PRICE OF TAHOE CONCEPTS?	11.00
HOW MANY SHARES OF TAHOE CONCEPTS ARE IN THE PORTFOLIO?	300
WHAT IS THE BETA FOR TAHOE CONCEPTS?	1.40
WHAT IS THE NAME OF STOCK 10?	NICHOLSON FINANCIAL
WHAT IS THE PRICE OF NICHOLSON FINANCIAL?	22.50
HOW MANY SHARES OF NICHOLSON FINANCIAL ARE IN THE PORTFOLIO?	500
WHAT IS THE BETA FOR NICHOLSON FINANCIAL?	1.25
WHAT IS THE NAME OF STOCK 11?	GLOBAL EXPLORATIONS
WHAT IS THE PRICE OF GLOBAL EXPLORATIONS?	39.00
HOW MANY SHARES OF GLOBAL EXPLORATIONS ARE IN THE PORTFOLIO?	200
WHAT IS THE BETA FOR GLOBAL EXPLORATIONS?	1.20
WHAT IS THE NAME OF STOCK 12?	AMERICAN FEDERATED
WHAT IS THE PRICE OF AMERICAN FEDERATED?	42.00
HOW MANY SHARES OF AMERICAN FEDERATED ARE IN THE PORTFOLIO?	500
WHAT IS THE BETA FOR AMERICAN FEDERATED?	1.35
WHAT IS THE RISK-FREE RATE?	10.9
WHAT IS THE EXPECTED RETURN ON THE MARKET?	14.2

At this point, the screen will clear, and the computer will provide the answer:

BETA OF THE PORTFOLIO
IS 1.48

THE EXPECTED RETURN OF
THE PORTFOLIO IS 15.78

THE TOTAL VALUE OF
THE PORTFOLIO IS
$ 104512.5

** DONE **

Now Mr. Singer wants to find the beta, expected rate of return, and total value of his portfolio if he sells Nuclear Medicine, Solar Energy, Hi-Tek Industries, and Lunar Radiographics. He wants to replace these stocks with 500 shares of General American. The value of the four stocks Mr. Singer will sell is actually high enough to buy 537 shares of General American, but due to brokerage commissions on the sale of the old stock and the purchase of the new stock, enough cash will remain to buy only 500 shares.

Let's run the program again, for the nine stocks that are now in Mr. Singer's portfolio:

Computer Request	Operator Input
HOW MANY STOCKS ARE IN THE PORTFOLIO?	9
WHAT IS THE NAME OF STOCK 1?	ADVANCE TECHNOLOGY
WHAT IS THE PRICE OF ADVANCE TECHNOLOGY?	22.00
HOW MANY SHARES OF ADVANCE TECHNOLOGY ARE IN THE PORTFOLIO?	500
WHAT IS THE BETA FOR ADVANCE TECHNOLOGY?	1.45
WHAT IS THE NAME OF STOCK 2?	OFFSHORE EXPLORATIONS
WHAT IS THE PRICE OF OFFSHORE EXPLORATIONS?	25.25
HOW MANY SHARES OF OFFSHORE EXPLORATIONS ARE IN THE PORTFOLIO?	100
WHAT IS THE BETA FOR OFFSHORE EXPLORATIONS?	1.50

Computer Request	Operator Input
WHAT IS THE NAME OF STOCK 3?	ALUMINUM RECYCLERS
WHAT IS THE PRICE OF ALUMINUM RECYCLERS?	47.00
HOW MANY SHARES OF ALUMINUM RECYCLERS ARE IN THE PORTFOLIO?	100
WHAT IS THE BETA FOR ALUMINUM RECYCLERS?	1.50
WHAT IS THE NAME OF STOCK 4?	OIL SERVICES
WHAT IS THE PRICE OF OIL SERVICES?	19.25
HOW MANY SHARES OF OIL SERVICES ARE IN THE PORTFOLIO?	500
WHAT IS THE BETA FOR OIL SERVICES?	1.30
WHAT IS THE NAME OF STOCK 5?	TAHOE CONCEPTS
WHAT IS THE PRICE OF TAHOE CONCEPTS?	11.00
HOW MANY SHARES OF TAHOE CONCEPTS ARE IN THE PORTFOLIO?	300
WHAT IS THE BETA FOR TAHOE CONCEPTS?	1.40
WHAT IS THE NAME OF STOCK 6?	NICHOLSON FINANCIAL
WHAT IS THE PRICE OF NICHOLSON FINANCIAL?	22.50
HOW MANY SHARES OF NICHOLSON FINANCIAL ARE IN THE PORTFOLIO?	500
WHAT IS THE BETA FOR NICHOLSON FINANCIAL?	1.25
WHAT IS THE NAME OF STOCK 7?	GLOBAL EXPLORATIONS
WHAT IS THE PRICE OF GLOBAL EXPLORATIONS?	39.00

Computer Request	Operator Input
HOW MANY SHARES OF GLOBAL EXPLORATIONS ARE IN THE PORTFOLIO?	200
WHAT IS THE BETA FOR GLOBAL EXPLORATIONS?	1.20
WHAT IS THE NAME OF STOCK 8?	AMERICAN FEDERATED
WHAT IS THE PRICE OF AMERICAN FEDERATED?	42.00
HOW MANY SHARES OF AMERICAN FEDERATED ARE IN THE PORTFOLIO?	500
WHAT IS THE BETA FOR AMERICAN FEDERATED?	1.35
WHAT IS THE NAME OF STOCK 9?	GENERAL AMERICAN
WHAT IS THE PRICE OF GENERAL AMERICAN?	62.00
HOW MANY SHARES OF GENERAL AMERICAN ARE IN THE PORTFOLIO?	500
WHAT IS THE BETA FOR GENERAL AMERICAN?	1.05
WHAT IS THE RISK-FREE RATE?	10.9
WHAT IS THE EXPECTED RETURN ON THE MARKET?	14.2

At this point, the screen will clear, and the computer will provide the answer:

BETA OF THE PORTFOLIO
IS 1.25

THE EXPECTED RETURN OF
THE PORTFOLIO IS 15.04

THE TOTAL VALUE OF
THE PORTFOLIO IS
$ 102200

** DONE **

As we can see from the two analyses, Mr. Singer would be lowering the expected rate of return in his portfolio only slightly if he sold the four riskiest stocks. At the same time, the riskiness of the portfolio would decrease significantly (from 1.48 to 1.25). For these reasons, replacing the risky stocks with General American stock is well-advised.

FORMULAS

The formulas are all included in the Program Listing; we'll review them here only for ease of reference.

TOTAL VALUE OF A PORTFOLIO

$$Q = \sum_{i=1}^{SP} P_i * SH_i \quad \text{(see program lines 330-340)}$$

where

Q = total value of portfolio
P_i = price of each stock in portfolio
SH_i = number of shares of each stock in portfolio
SP = number of shares in portfolio

BETA OF A PORTFOLIO

$$BP = \sum_{i=1}^{SP} PT_i * B_i \quad \text{(see program lines 370 to 380)}$$

where

BP = beta of a portfolio
PT_i = percent of each stock in portfolio
B_i = beta of each stock in portfolio
SP = number of shares in portfolio

EXPECTED RETURN OF A PORTFOLIO

$$K = RF + BP*(KM - RF) \quad \text{(see program line 480)}$$

where

K = expected return of a portfolio
RF = risk-free rate of return
BP = beta of a portfolio
KM = expected return on market

PROGRAM LISTING

PORTFOLIO ANALYSIS

```
100 CALL CLEAR
110 DIM P(50),A$(50),SH(50),Q(50),PT(50),B(50)
120 PRINT "HOW MANY STOCKS ARE"
130 PRINT "IN THE PORTFOLIO";
140 INPUT SP
150 FOR I=1 TO SP
160 PRINT
170 PRINT "WHAT IS THE NAME OF"
180 PRINT "STOCK";I;
190 INPUT A$(I)
200 PRINT
210 PRINT "WHAT IS THE PRICE OF"
220 PRINT A$(I);
230 INPUT P(I)
240 PRINT
250 PRINT "HOW MANY SHARES OF"
260 PRINT A$(I)
270 PRINT "ARE IN THE PORTFOLIO";
280 INPUT SH(I)
290 PRINT
300 PRINT "WHAT IS THE BETA FOR"
310 PRINT A$(I);
320 INPUT B(I)
330 Q(I)=P(I)*SH(I)
340 QT=QT+Q(I)
350 NEXT I
360 FOR I=1 TO SP
370 PT(I)=Q(I)/QT
380 BP=BP+PT(I)*B(I)
390 NEXT I
400 PRINT
410 PRINT "WHAT IS THE RISK-FREE"
420 PRINT "RATE";
430 INPUT RF
440 PRINT
450 PRINT "WHAT IS THE EXPECTED"
460 PRINT "RETURN ON THE MARKET";
470 INPUT KM
480 K=RF+BP*(KM-RF)
490 CALL CLEAR
500 PRINT "BETA OF THE PORTFOLIO"
```

Note: If using the TI Professional Computer, substitute PRINT CHR$(12) for CALL CLEAR.

Berk & Berk: Financial Analysis with Texas Instruments Microcomputers (Chilton)

```
510 PRINT "IS";INT((BP+.005)*100)/100
520 PRINT
530 PRINT "THE EXPECTED RETURN OF"
540 PRINT "THE PORTFOLIO IS";INT((K+.005)*100)/100
550 PRINT
560 PRINT "THE TOTAL VALUE OF"
570 PRINT "THE PORTFOLIO IS"
580 PRINT "$ ";QT
590 END
```

Discount Analysis
11

Wholesalers frequently offer a discount to businesses that pay their bills early. Typically, the discount terms are expressed in the following manner: 2/10 net 30. This means the wholesaler will allow a 2 percent discount if the purchaser pays within 10 days. If the purchasing business takes longer than 10 days to pay, it cannot take the discount. In that case, the business must pay the full amount within 30 days.

Most people would interpret the above as a 2 percent annual discount, but that is not correct. Actually, the purchaser is being offered a 2 percent discount every time an order is placed. In practical terms, this means that the purchasing business must pay more if it does not take advantage of the discount.

The Discount Analysis program allows us to determine the true cost (on an annualized percentage basis) of not taking advantage of early payment discounts. The following example will illustrate this concept.

SAMPLE ANALYSIS: COUNTING A DISCOUNT

Reggie's Tavern has just received a shipment of beer. The invoice asks for payment of $600.00, with terms of 4/25 net 60. Reggie knows he will receive a 4 percent discount if he pays the bill within 25 days. If he waits longer than 25 days to pay, he must pay the full amount within 60 days. What is Reggie's annualized cost of not taking the discount?

We can answer this question with discount analysis. Load the program (listed on page 116) into the TI-99/4A, enter the command RUN, and here's what the computer will ask for:

Computer Request	Operator Input
WHAT IS THE DISCOUNT (EXPRESSED AS A PERCENT)?	4
IN HOW MANY DAYS MUST THE BILL BE PAID TO RECEIVE THE DISCOUNT?	25
WHAT IS THE MAXIMUM NUMBER OF DAYS IN WHICH THE BILL MUST BE PAID?	60

At this point, the screen will clear, and the computer will display the answer:

THE ANNUALIZED COST OF
NOT TAKING THE DISCOUNT IS
43.45 PERCENT
OF THE AMOUNT DUE

** DONE **

FORMULA

The formula is included in the Program Listing, and is reviewed here for your reference.

ANNUALIZED COST OF NOT TAKING A DISCOUNT

$$D = A/(1 - A)*365/(C - B)$$ (see program line 290)

where

D = annualized cost of not taking a discount
A = stated discount
B = number of days in which bill must be paid to receive discount
C = maximum number of days in which bill must be paid

PROGRAM LISTING

DISCOUNT ANALYSIS

```
100 CALL CLEAR
110 PRINT "WHAT IS THE DISCOUNT"
120 PRINT "(EXPRESSED AS A"
130 PRINT "PERCENT)";
140 INPUT A
150 A=A/100
160 PRINT
170 PRINT "IN HOW MANY DAYS MUST"
180 PRINT "THE BILL BE PAID"
190 PRINT "TO RECEIVE THE"
200 PRINT "DISCOUNT";
210 INPUT B
220 PRINT
230 PRINT "WHAT IS THE MAXIMUM"
240 PRINT "NUMBER OF DAYS IN"
250 PRINT "WHICH THE BILL"
260 PRINT "MUST BE PAID";
270 INPUT C
280 CALL CLEAR
290 D=A/(1-A)*365/(C-B)
300 PRINT "THE ANNUALIZED COST OF"
310 PRINT "NOT TAKING THE DISCOUNT IS"
320 PRINT INT((D+.00005)*10000)/100;" PERCENT"
330 PRINT "OF THE AMOUNT DUE"
340 END
```

Note: If using the TI Professional Computer, substitute PRINT CHR$(12) for CALL CLEAR.

Effective Annual Interest Rate Analysis
12

Interest is the amount of money earned by money invested. The rate of interest is often expressed on an annualized basis, even though this frequently misrepresents the true, or effective annual, interest rate. This is due to the effect of compounding (or earning interest on interest).

Most financial institutions use compounding periods that occur more often than once a year (even though they express the interest rate on an annual basis). Compounding periods may occur at six-month, quarterly, monthly, weekly, or even daily intervals. For some theoretical applications, interest may even be treated as if it compounded continuously. The shorter the compounding period, the greater the effective rate of interest, because the interest then earns interest more frequently. Determining the effective annual interest rate can provide a useful standard of comparison when making investment decisions.

SAMPLE ANALYSIS: EARNING INTEREST ON INTEREST

Suppose you wish to place a sum of money in a savings account. After contacting several financial institutions, you find three that pay 10 percent interest. The first bank has a six-month compounding period, the second has a quarterly compounding period, and the third has a daily compounding period. Being an astute investor, you want to earn the maximum interest on your money.

Let's use the TI-99/4A to solve this problem. Load the Effective Annual Interest Rate program (the listing begins on page 123), enter the command RUN, and here's what the computer will ask for:

Computer Request	Operator Input
WHAT IS THE NOMINAL (OR STATED) ANNUAL INTEREST RATE?	10
WHAT IS THE COMPOUNDING PERIOD? ENTER	
A FOR CONTINUOUS	
B FOR DAILY	
C FOR WEEKLY	
D FOR MONTHLY	
E FOR QUARTERLY	
F FOR SEMI-ANNUALLY	
G FOR ANNUALLY	
?	F

After you've entered the above data, the computer will print out:

THE EFFECTIVE ANNUAL
INTEREST RATE IS
10.25 PERCENT

** DONE **

This shows that even though the stated interest rate is 10 percent, we actually earn a little more, because the interest compounds at six-month intervals. Let's now run the analysis for the second bank, which offers quarterly compounding. Enter the command RUN again, and here's what the computer will ask for:

Computer Request	Operator Input
WHAT IS THE NOMINAL (OR STATED) ANNUAL INTEREST RATE?	10
WHAT IS THE COMPOUNDING PERIOD? ENTER	
A FOR CONTINUOUS	
B FOR DAILY	
C FOR WEEKLY	
D FOR MONTHLY	

Computer Request	Operator Input
E FOR QUARTERLY F FOR SEMI-ANNUALLY G FOR ANNUALLY	
?	E

After you've entered the above data, the computer will print out:

THE EFFECTIVE ANNUAL
INTEREST RATE IS
10.38128906 PERCENT

** DONE **

We can see from this run that when the interest is compounded quarterly, the effective annual interest rate is a little bit higher than when the interest is compounded only twice a year. Money deposited in the bank offering quarterly compounding will earn more because the effective annual interest rate is greater.

Let's now run the analysis for the third bank, which has a daily compounding period. Enter the command RUN, and here's what the computer will ask for:

Computer Request	Operator Input
WHAT IS THE NOMINAL (OR STATED) ANNUAL INTEREST RATE?	10
WHAT IS THE COMPOUNDING PERIOD?	
ENTER	

A FOR CONTINUOUS
    B FOR DAILY
    C FOR WEEKLY
    D FOR MONTHLY
    E FOR QUARTERLY
    F FOR SEMI-ANNUALLY
    G FOR ANNUALLY	

?	B

After you've entered the above data, the computer will print out:

THE EFFECTIVE ANNUAL
INTEREST RATE IS
10.51557817 PERCENT

** DONE **

Daily compounding, as we can see from the above answer, provides the greatest return on your investment. That's because the effective annual interest rate is higher than either semi-annual or quarterly compounding provides. The best investment, therefore, would be to deposit your money in the third bank.

As a point of interest, let's see what the annual interest rate would be if the continuous compounding is used. Enter the command RUN, and here's what the computer will ask for:

Computer Request	Operator Input
WHAT IS THE NOMINAL (OR STATED) ANNUAL INTEREST RATE?	10
WHAT IS THE COMPOUNDING PERIOD	
ENTER	
A FOR CONTINUOUS	
B FOR DAILY	
C FOR WEEKLY	
D FOR MONTHLY	
E FOR QUARTERLY	
F FOR SEMI-ANNUALLY	
G FOR ANNUALLY	
?	A

At this point, the screen will clear, and the computer will display the answer:

THE EFFECTIVE ANNUAL
INTEREST RATE IS
10.51709781 PERCENT

** DONE **

Our example shows that when the interest rates are all the same, a shorter compounding period provides a greater return. Continuous compounding provides the highest effective annual interest rate. We can see, though, that daily compounding provides an effective annual interest rate that is very close to the rate provided by continuous compounding (10.51557817 percent for daily compounding, versus 10.5170981 percent for continuous compounding).

In the problem we just finished, we examined the effects of different compounding periods on the same nominal interest rate. But what happens when the interest rates and compounding periods are both different? This is when the computer can really help, as the following example shows.

SAMPLE ANALYSIS: VARIABLE INTEREST AND COMPOUNDING RATES

Suppose you are faced with a choice similar to the one in the first example, except now you have only two banks to consider. The first bank pays 12 percent interest, compounded annually. The second bank pays 11.5 percent, but this bank offers monthly compounding. Which bank has the higher effective annual interest rate?

Let's run the Effective Annual Interest Rate program to find the answer. Here's how it looks for the first bank:

Computer Request	Operator Input
WHAT IS THE NOMINAL (OR STATED) ANNUAL INTEREST RATE?	12
WHAT IS THE COMPOUNDING PERIOD? ENTER	
A FOR CONTINUOUS	
B FOR DAILY	
C FOR WEEKLY	
D FOR MONTHLY	
E FOR QUARTERLY	
F FOR SEMI-ANNUALLY	
G FOR ANNUALLY	
?	G

Once the above data has been entered, the answer will appear:

THE EFFECTIVE ANNUAL
INTEREST RATE IS
12 PERCENT

** DONE **

The computer shows that the bank paying 12 percent interest (with an annual compounding period) has an effective annual interest rate of exactly 12 percent. This is as we would expect, since the compounding period is one year.

Now let's run the analysis for the second bank, which offers monthly compounding on 11.5 percent interest. Enter the command RUN, and here's what the computer will ask for:

Computer Request	Operator Input
WHAT IS THE NOMINAL (OR STATED) ANNUAL INTEREST RATE?	11.5

Computer Request	Operator Input
WHAT IS THE COMPOUNDING PERIOD?	
ENTER	
A FOR CONTINUOUS	
B FOR DAILY	
C FOR WEEKLY	
D FOR MONTHLY	
E FOR QUARTERLY	
F FOR SEMI-ANNUALLY	
G FOR ANNUALLY	
?	D

After you've entered the above data, the computer will print out:

THE EFFECTIVE ANNUAL
INTEREST RATE IS
12.12593281 PERCENT

** DONE **

In this case, we find that the bank paying 11.5 percent interest (compounded monthly) has an effective annual interest rate of 12.12593281 percent. This is higher than that of the bank offering 12 percent interest with annual compounding. Therefore, you would earn more money by opening an account at the bank paying 11.5 percent!

FORMULAS

Formulas are included in the Program Listing; they are reviewed here for ease of reference.

EFFECTIVE ANNUAL INTEREST RATE FOR
CONTINUOUS COMPOUNDING

$$APR = EXP(I) - 1 \quad \text{(see program line 410)}$$

where

APR = effective annual interest rate
$EXP(I)$ = e raised to the Ith power
I = nominal, or stated, annual interest rate

EFFECTIVE ANNUAL INTEREST RATE FOR OTHER THAN CONTINUOUS COMPOUNDING

$$APR = (1 + I/M)^M - 1 \quad \text{(see program line 540)}$$

where

APR = effective annual interest rate
I = nominal, or stated, annual interest rate
M = compounding period

The implicit assumption in the above formula is that the frequency of calculating and crediting interest coincides with the compounding period.

PROGRAM LISTING

EFFECTIVE ANNUAL INTEREST RATE ANALYSIS

```
100 CALL CLEAR
110 PRINT "WHAT IS THE NOMINAL"
120 PRINT "(OR STATED) ANNUAL"
130 PRINT "INTEREST RATE";
140 INPUT I
150 I = I/100
160 PRINT
170 PRINT "WHAT IS THE"
180 PRINT "COMPOUNDING PERIOD"
190 PRINT
200 PRINT
210 PRINT "ENTER"
220 PRINT
230 PRINT
240 PRINT TAB(5);"A FOR CONTINUOUS"
250 PRINT TAB(5);"B FOR DAILY"
260 PRINT TAB(5);"C FOR WEEKLY"
270 PRINT TAB(5);"D FOR MONTHLY"
280 PRINT TAB(5);"E FOR QUARTERLY"
290 PRINT TAB(5);"F FOR SEMI-ANNUALLY"
300 PRINT TAB(5);"G FOR ANNUALLY"
310 PRINT
320 INPUT AN$
330 IF AN$ = "A" THEN 410
340 IF AN$ = "B" THEN 430
350 IF AN$ = "C" THEN 450
360 IF AN$ = "D" THEN 470
```

Note: If using the TI Professional Computer, substitute PRINT CHR$(12) for CALL CLEAR.

```
370 IF AN$="E" THEN 490
380 IF AN$="F" THEN 510
390 IF AN$="G" THEN 530
400 GO TO 170
410 APR=EXP(I)-1
420 GO TO 550
430 M=365
440 GO TO 540
450 M=52
460 GO TO 540
470 M=12
480 GO TO 540
490 M=4
500 GO TO 540
510 M=2
520 GO TO 540
530 M=1
540 APR=(1+I/M)∧M-1
550 CALL CLEAR
560 PRINT "THE EFFECTIVE ANNUAL"
570 PRINT "INTEREST RATE IS"
580 PRINT APR*100;"PERCENT"
590 END
```

Future Value Analysis
13

One of the most interesting financial management concepts is the time value of money. Money is invested today so that it will be worth more tomorrow.

To illustrate this concept, suppose you inherited $10,000 and decided to hide it under your mattress. One year from now, if you took the money out, it would still be worth only $10,000. The money didn't grow in value because your mattress pays no interest.

Suppose that instead you put it into an interest-bearing account. You know the money will draw interest and the size of the account will grow. Future value analysis allows you to determine exactly how much the account will be worth at any time in the future, given that you know the interest rate and the compounding period.

SAMPLE ANALYSIS: A 5-YEAR CD

Let's take the same $10,000 we used above, and invest it in a five-year time certificate of deposit. The certificate pays 13.5 percent interest, compounded daily. We'd like to know the value of the account at the end of the five years.

Load the Future Value Analysis program beginning on page 128 into your TI-99/4A, enter the command RUN, and here's what the computer will ask for:

Computer Request	Operator Input
WHAT IS THE PRESENT VALUE?	10000
WHAT IS THE ANNUAL INTEREST RATE?	13.5
WHAT IS THE COMPOUNDING PERIOD? ENTER	
365 FOR DAILY	
52 FOR WEEKLY	
12 FOR MONTHLY	
4 FOR QUARTERLY	
2 FOR SEMI-ANNUALLY	
1 FOR ANNUALLY	
?	365
HOW MANY YEARS FROM NOW DO YOU WISH TO CALCULATE FUTURE VALUE?	5

Once you've entered the above data, the screen will clear, and the computer will provide the answer:

FUTURE VALUE = $19637.88

** DONE **

To show the effect of compounding interest at less than a daily rate, run the analysis again, but use a quarterly compounding period. You'll see that at the end of five years, the difference between an account that compounds quarterly and one that compounds daily will be over $200!

SAMPLE ANALYSIS: PAY NOW/PAY LATER?

Atlas Industries builds ships for the Navy. During contract negotiations for a new ship, the Navy offers to pay Atlas either one million dollars today (at the start of construction), or two million dollars when the ship is completed (at the end of four years). If Atlas can earn 15 percent effective annual interest on its money by investing in other areas, which is the best offer?

Future value analysis makes this an easy problem to solve, because it gives us a standard of comparison. We can determine how much the million dollars will be worth in four years, and see if the future value exceeds the two million dollars the Navy is willing to pay then.

Let's run the Future Value Analysis program for a million dollars invested for four years at 15 percent interest (compounded annually, since the 15 percent is an effective annual interest rate). Load the program into your TI-99/4A, enter the command RUN, and here's what the computer will ask for:

Computer Request	Operator Input
WHAT IS THE PRESENT VALUE?	1000000
WHAT IS THE ANNUAL INTEREST RATE?	15

WHAT IS THE COMPOUNDING PERIOD?
ENTER
    365 FOR DAILY
    52 FOR WEEKLY
    12 FOR MONTHLY
    4 FOR QUARTERLY
    2 FOR SEMI-ANNUALLY
    1 FOR ANNUALLY
?
	1

HOW MANY YEARS FROM NOW DO YOU WISH TO CALCULATE FUTURE VALUE?	4

Once you've entered the above data, the screen will clear, and the computer will provide the answer:

FUTURE VALUE = $1749006.25

** DONE **

The computer shows us that in four years the million dollars will be worth $1,749,006.25. This is less than the two million dollars the Navy is willing to pay then. If Atlas can wait four years to get paid (and the company is sure it can build good ships so there will be no contract disputes), it should opt for the deferred payment of two million dollars.

FORMULA

The formula is included in the Program Listing, and is reviewed here only for reference.

FUTURE VALUE

$$FV = PV*(1 + I/CP)^N \quad \text{(see program lines 410 to 430)}$$

where

FV = future value
PV = present value
I = nominal, or stated, annual interest rate
CP = compounding period
N = number of compounding periods

The implicit assumption in the above formula is that the frequency of calculating and crediting interest coincides with the compounding period.

PROGRAM LISTING

FUTURE VALUE ANALYSIS

```
100 CALL CLEAR
110 PRINT "WHAT IS THE"
120 PRINT "PRESENT VALUE";
130 INPUT PV
140 PRINT
150 PRINT "WHAT IS THE"
160 PRINT "ANNUAL INTEREST RATE";
170 INPUT I
180 I=I/100
190 CALL CLEAR
200 PRINT "WHAT IS THE"
210 PRINT "COMPOUNDING PERIOD?"
220 PRINT
230 PRINT
240 PRINT "ENTER"
250 PRINT
260 PRINT TAB(5);"365 FOR DAILY"
270 PRINT TAB(5);"52 FOR WEEKLY"
280 PRINT TAB(5);"12 FOR MONTHLY"
290 PRINT TAB(5);"4 FOR QUARTERLY"
300 PRINT TAB(5);"2 FOR SEMI-ANNUALLY"
310 PRINT TAB(5);"1 FOR ANNUALLY"
320 PRINT
330 PRINT
340 INPUT CP
```

Note: If using the TI Professional Computer, substitute PRINT CHR$(12) for CALL CLEAR.

Berk & Berk: Financial Analysis with Texas Instruments Microcomputers (Chilton)

```
350 CALL CLEAR
360 PRINT "HOW MANY YEARS FROM"
370 PRINT "NOW DO YOU WISH"
380 PRINT "TO CALCULATE"
390 PRINT "FUTURE VALUE";
400 INPUT P
410 N = INT(P*CP)
420 K = I/CP
430 FV = PV*(1+K)∧N
440 FV = INT((FV+.005)*100)/100
450 CALL CLEAR
460 PRINT "FUTURE VALUE = $";FV
470 END
```

Future Value of an Annuity Analysis
14

In the previous section, we explored the concept of future value for a fixed amount of money. In this section, we'll examine how to determine the future value of a series of payments.

A series of payments is commonly referred to as an annuity, even though the payments need not occur on an annual basis. The payments may be made daily, weekly, monthly, quarterly, or at any other regular time interval.

Several payment situations will be addressed in this section. We'll examine how to determine the future value of a regular series of payments, and assess the effects of different interest rates and compounding periods. Then we'll take a look at more complex payment schedules, where the amount of the payment will vary.

SAMPLE ANALYSIS: PAYROLL SAVINGS

Your company offers a payroll savings plan. The plan automatically deducts $10 from your pay each week and deposits the money into a special savings account. The plan pays 9.75 percent interest (compounded monthly); how much will your account be worth at the end of the first, second, and third years?

Load the Future Value of an Annuity program into your TI-99/4A (the listing begins on page 137), enter the command RUN, and here's what the computer will ask for:

Computer Request	Operator Input
WHAT IS THE PERIODIC PAYMENT?	10
HOW OFTEN IS IT MADE?	
ENTER	
365 FOR DAILY	
52 FOR WEEKLY	
12 FOR MONTHLY	
4 FOR QUARTERLY	
2 FOR SEMI-ANNUALLY	
1 FOR ANNUALLY	
?	52
WHAT IS THE INTEREST RATE?	9.75
WHAT IS THE INTEREST COMPOUNDING PERIOD?	
ENTER	
365 FOR DAILY	
52 FOR WEEKLY	
12 FOR MONTHLY	
4 FOR QUARTERLY	
2 FOR SEMI-ANNUALLY	
1 FOR ANNUALLY	
?	12
FOR HOW MANY YEARS WILL PAYMENTS BE MADE?	1

At this point, the screen will clear and the computer will provide the answer for the first year:

FUTURE VALUE = $543.88

** DONE **

This is only part of the answer, though. We now need to run the program for two and three years to find the value of the annuity at the end of these periods. Let's do the analysis for two years first:

Computer Request	Operator Input
WHAT IS THE PERIODIC PAYMENT?	10
HOW OFTEN IS IT MADE?	

Computer Request	Operator Input
ENTER	
365 FOR DAILY	
52 FOR WEEKLY	
12 FOR MONTHLY	
4 FOR QUARTERLY	
2 FOR SEMI-ANNUALLY	
1 FOR ANNUALLY	
?	52
WHAT IS THE INTEREST RATE?	9.75
WHAT IS THE INTEREST COMPOUNDING PERIOD?	
ENTER	
365 FOR DAILY	
52 FOR WEEKLY	
12 FOR MONTHLY	
4 FOR QUARTERLY	
2 FOR SEMI-ANNUALLY	
1 FOR ANNUALLY	
?	12
FOR HOW MANY YEARS WILL PAYMENTS BE MADE?	2

Once we've entered this data, the screen will clear, and the computer will provide the answer:

FUTURE VALUE = $1143.22

** DONE **

Let's run the program one more time to find out how much the annuity will be worth at the end of the third year.

Computer Request	Operator Input
WHAT IS THE PERIODIC PAYMENT?	10
HOW OFTEN IS IT MADE?	
ENTER	
365 FOR DAILY	
52 FOR WEEKLY	
12 FOR MONTHLY	
4 FOR QUARTERLY	

Computer Request	Operator Input
2 FOR SEMI-ANNUALLY	
1 FOR ANNUALLY	
?	52
WHAT IS THE INTEREST RATE?	9.75
WHAT IS THE INTEREST COMPOUNDING PERIOD?	
ENTER	
365 FOR DAILY	
52 FOR WEEKLY	
12 FOR MONTHLY	
4 FOR QUARTERLY	
2 FOR SEMI-ANNUALLY	
1 FOR ANNUALLY	
?	12
FOR HOW MANY YEARS WILL PAYMENTS BE MADE?	3

Once again, the screen will clear, and the computer will provide the answer:

FUTURE VALUE = $1803.68

** DONE **

From the above runs, we now know the value of the annuity at the end of the first, second, and third years will be $543.88, $1143.22, and $1803.68.

SAMPLE ANALYSIS: CALCULATING TWO ANNUITIES

The Daisy Hill Gift Shop is a seasonal business. Profit is fairly consistent for eleven months out of the year, but jumps to about four times normal during the month of December due to holiday sales. Donna Jones, the owner, would like to start a savings plan. She plans to deposit $100 every month for January through November, and $400 in December. If Ms. Jones' savings account pays 11 percent interest (compounded quarterly), how much will the account be worth at the end of five years?

We are really dealing with two annuities in this problem. The first is a regular series of monthly $100 payments. The second annuity is a regular series of annual $300 payments. The annual payment mentioned in the description of the problem is $400, but we're going to think of $100 of it as being part of the regular monthly annuity. That leaves $300 for the annual payment.

Once we've structured the problem this way, the solution is straightforward. We simply use the computer to find the future value of the $100 monthly annuity, and then do the same for the $300 annual annuity. The sum of these two annuities will be the future value of the series of payments at the end of five years. Let's run the two analyses to find the value of each annuity. We'll do the $100 monthly annuity first.

Computer Request	Operator Input
WHAT IS THE PERIODIC PAYMENT?	100
HOW OFTEN IS IT MADE?	
ENTER	
365 FOR DAILY	
52 FOR WEEKLY	
12 FOR MONTHLY	
4 FOR QUARTERLY	
2 FOR SEMI-ANNUALLY	
1 FOR ANNUALLY	
?	12
WHAT IS THE INTEREST RATE?	11
WHAT IS THE INTEREST COMPOUNDING PERIOD?	
ENTER	
365 FOR DAILY	
52 FOR WEEKLY	
12 FOR MONTHLY	
4 FOR QUARTERLY	
2 FOR SEMI-ANNUALLY	
1 FOR ANNUALLY	
?	4
FOR HOW MANY YEARS WILL PAYMENTS BE MADE?	5

After we've entered the above data, the computer will tell us the future value of the $100 monthly annuity at the end of five years.

FUTURE VALUE = $7859.22

** DONE **

Now we need to run the program again, but this time we'll find the future value of the $300 annual annuity.

Computer Request	Operator Input
WHAT IS THE PERIODIC PAYMENT?	300
HOW OFTEN IS IT MADE?	
ENTER	
365 FOR DAILY	
52 FOR WEEKLY	
12 FOR MONTHLY	
4 FOR QUARTERLY	
2 FOR SEMI-ANNUALLY	
1 FOR ANNUALLY	
?	1
WHAT IS THE INTEREST RATE?	11
WHAT IS THE INTEREST COMPOUNDING PERIOD?	
ENTER	
365 FOR DAILY	
52 FOR WEEKLY	
12 FOR MONTHLY	
4 FOR QUARTERLY	
2 FOR SEMI-ANNUALLY	
1 FOR ANNUALLY	
?	4
FOR HOW MANY YEARS WILL PAYMENTS BE MADE?	5

When we finish entering the above data, the screen will clear, and the computer will provide the future value of the $300 annual annuity:

FUTURE VALUE = $1885.59

** DONE **

Now that we have the future values of the $100 monthly annuity ($7859.22) and the $300 annual annuity ($1885.59), we merely need to add them together to find the future value of Ms. Jones' savings account. This amount is $9744.81, which represents the future value of the series of payments at the end of five years.

FORMULAS

Formulas are included in the Program Listing; they are reviewed here for your reference.

FUTURE VALUE OF AN ANNUITY

If the periodic payment occurs at the same time as, or more often than, the compounding period:

$$FV = PP \sum_{i=0}^{N-1} (1 + I/CP)^{J_i} \text{ (see program lines 520 and 560 to 590)}$$

If the periodic payment occurs less frequently than the compounding period:

$$FV = PP \sum_{i=0}^{P*T-1} (1 + I/CP)^{(J_i*CP/T)} \text{ (see program lines 520 and 610 to 630)}$$

where

FV = future value of an annuity
PP = periodic payment
I = nominal, or stated, annual interest rate
CP = compounding period
N = number of compounding periods
J_i = number of compounding period
T = number of payments per year
P = number of years

The implicit assumption in the above formulas is that the frequency of calculating and crediting interest coincides with the compounding period.

PROGRAM LISTING

FUTURE VALUE OF AN ANNUITY ANALYSIS

```
100 CALL CLEAR
110 PRINT "WHAT IS THE PERIODIC"
120 PRINT "PAYMENT";
130 INPUT PP
140 PRINT
150 PRINT "HOW OFTEN IS IT MADE?"
160 PRINT
170 PRINT
180 PRINT "ENTER"
190 PRINT
200 PRINT TAB(5);"365 FOR DAILY"
210 PRINT TAB(5);"52 FOR WEEKLY"
220 PRINT TAB(5);"12 FOR MONTHLY"
230 PRINT TAB(5);"4 FOR QUARTERLY"
240 PRINT TAB(5);"2 FOR SEMI-ANNUALLY"
250 PRINT TAB(5);"1 FOR ANNUALLY"
260 PRINT
270 INPUT T
280 CALL CLEAR
290 PRINT "WHAT IS THE"
300 PRINT "INTEREST RATE";
310 INPUT I
320 PRINT
330 I = I/100
340 PRINT "WHAT IS THE INTEREST"
350 PRINT "COMPOUNDING PERIOD?"
360 PRINT
370 PRINT
380 PRINT "ENTER"
390 PRINT
400 PRINT TAB(5);"365 FOR DAILY"
410 PRINT TAB(5);"52 FOR WEEKLY"
420 PRINT TAB(5);"12 FOR MONTHLY"
430 PRINT TAB(5);"4 FOR QUARTERLY"
440 PRINT TAB(5);"2 FOR SEMI-ANNUALLY"
450 PRINT TAB(5);"1 FOR ANNUALLY"
460 PRINT
470 INPUT CP
480 PRINT
490 PRINT "FOR HOW MANY YEARS WILL"
500 PRINT "PAYMENTS BE MADE";
```

Note: If using the TI Professional Computer, substitute PRINT CHR$(12) for CALL CLEAR.

```
510 INPUT P
520 K=I/CP
530 N=INT(CP*P)
540 FV=0
550 IF T<CP THEN 610
560 PP=PP*(T/CP)
570 FOR J=0 TO N-1
580 FV= FV+PP*(1+K)^J
590 NEXT J
600 GO TO 640
610 FOR J=0 TO P*T-1
620 FV=FV+PP*(1+K)^((CP/T)*J)
630 NEXT J
640 FV=INT((FV+.005)*100)/100
650 CALL CLEAR
660 PRINT "FUTURE VALUE = $";FV
670 END
```

Present Value Analysis
15

In the last two chapters we addressed the concept of future value; now we're going to learn about the concept of present value. As you may have guessed, we're going to find out how much a specified amount of money in the future is worth today.

This concept is useful both to the small investor and the corporate financial analyst. The small investor may want to determine how much money to invest today to reach a specified amount tomorrow, or he may want to evaluate different investments to find the one that requires the lowest cash outlay to reach a specified amount in the future. We'll look at two examples to illustrate these concepts. Our discussion on using present value analysis for corporate investment decisions will be deferred to Chapter 18, Net Present Value Analysis.

SAMPLE ANALYSIS: INVESTING NOW FOR A FIXED RETURN

Bob Meade wants to find out how much money he should deposit in his bank so that the account will grow to $5,000 at the end of three years. Mr. Meade's bank pays 9 percent interest, compounded monthly.

Let's solve this problem for Mr. Meade. Load the Present Value Analysis program into the TI-99/4A (the listing is on page 144), enter the command RUN, and here's what the computer will ask for:

Computer Request	Operator Input
WHAT IS THE FUTURE VALUE?	5000
WHAT IS THE ANNUAL INTEREST RATE?	9
WHAT IS THE COMPOUNDING PERIOD? ENTER	
365 FOR DAILY	
52 FOR WEEKLY	
12 FOR MONTHLY	
4 FOR QUARTERLY	
2 FOR SEMI-ANNUALLY	
1 FOR ANNUALLY	
?	12
HOW MANY YEARS FROM NOW IS THE FUTURE VALUE?	3

Once you've entered the above data, the screen will clear, and the computer will provide the answer:

PRESENT VALUE = $3820.74

** DONE **

SAMPLE ANALYSIS: DETERMINING SMALLEST PRESENT VALUE

Ed Johnson wants to buy an expensive car when he retires in six years. He has good reason to believe the purchase price of the car will be $27,000 at that time, including all tax, title, and licensing fees. Mr. Johnson wants to put enough money in the bank today so that when he retires, the money will have grown to $27,000.

After checking several investment options, Mr. Johnson has narrowed his choice to three savings and loan associations. Western Savings pays 10%, compounded quarterly. American Financial offers a slightly lower rate (9.75%), but the interest is compounded daily. First Federated offers the highest interest (12%), but the interest is only compounded every six months. Which represents the best choice for Mr. Johnson, who wants the investment requiring the lowest cash outlay? He should select the investment option that provides the smallest present value for the $27,000 it will take to buy the new car in six years.

With that in mind, let's run the analysis for the three savings and loan associations. We'll do Western Savings first. Load the program into the TI-99/4A, enter the command RUN, and here's what the computer will ask for:

Computer Request	Operator Input
WHAT IS THE FUTURE VALUE?	27000
WHAT IS THE ANNUAL INTEREST RATE?	10
WHAT IS THE COMPOUNDING PERIOD? ENTER	
365 FOR DAILY	
52 FOR WEEKLY	
12 FOR MONTHLY	
4 FOR QUARTERLY	
2 FOR SEMI-ANNUALLY	
1 FOR ANNUALLY	
?	4
HOW MANY YEARS FROM NOW IS THE FUTURE VALUE?	6

Once you've entered the above data, the screen will clear, and the computer will provide the answer:

PRESENT VALUE = $14927.63

** DONE **

Now let's take a look at American Financial, and see how much Mr. Johnson will have to deposit to reach $27,000 in six years. Enter the command RUN, and here's what the computer will ask for:

Computer Request	Operator Input
WHAT IS THE FUTURE VALUE?	27000
WHAT IS THE ANNUAL INTEREST RATE?	9.75

Computer Request	Operator Input
WHAT IS THE COMPOUNDING PERIOD?	
ENTER	
365 FOR DAILY	
52 FOR WEEKLY	
12 FOR MONTHLY	
4 FOR QUARTERLY	
2 FOR SEMI-ANNUALLY	
1 FOR ANNUALLY	
?	365
HOW MANY YEARS FROM NOW IS THE FUTURE VALUE	6

At this point, the screen will clear, and the computer will provide the answer:

PRESENT VALUE = $15043.03

** DONE **

The last thing we need to do is run the program one more time for First Federated. Here's how it looks:

Computer Request	Operator Input
WHAT IS THE FUTURE VALUE?	27000
WHAT IS THE ANNUAL INTEREST RATE?	12
WHAT IS THE COMPOUNDING PERIOD?	
ENTER	
365 FOR DAILY	
52 FOR WEEKLY	
12 FOR MONTHLY	
4 FOR QUARTERLY	
2 FOR SEMI-ANNUALLY	
1 FOR ANNUALLY	
?	2
HOW MANY YEARS FROM NOW IS THE FUTURE VALUE?	6

After the above data has been entered, the computer will give us the answer for First Federated:

PRESENT VALUE = $13418.17
** DONE **

Since investing in First Federated requires the smallest present value, that's where Mr. Johnson should deposit his money. He'll need to invest only $13,418.17 to have $27,000 in six years. The other two savings and loan associations require a larger initial investment.

This example illustrates a concept that many people at first find confusing. First Federated, which pays the highest interest, requires the lowest initial investment. This is opposite to what we might expect, because we usually associate the highest interest rate with the largest sum of money. For this application, though, we want to minimize the present value of a specified amount in the future. The investment vehicle with the highest effective annual interest will allow the smallest investment today to reach the future amount. That's why, in this example, the highest interest rate is associated with the lowest dollar amount.

Now that we're becoming skilled financial analysts (along with the help of the TI), we can run two interesting checks on the answers we obtained for this problem. The first is to calculate the effective annual interest rate for the three savings and loan associations. We'd expect Western Savings to have the highest effective annual interest rate, since money deposited there shows the greatest growth. Run the Effective Annual Interest program, and see if this is true. The other check we can run is to work the problem backwards with the Future Value Analysis program. Try running the present values we obtained (at the interest and compounding periods for each) and see whether the answer equals the future value of $27,000.

FORMULA

The formula is included in the Program Listing, and reviewed here for your reference.

PRESENT VALUE

$$PV = FV/(1 + I/CP)^N \quad \text{(see program lines 410–430)}$$

where

PV = present value
FV = future value
I = nominal, or stated, annual interest rate
CP = compounding period
N = number of compounding periods

The implicit assumption in the above formula is that the frequency of calculating and crediting interest coincides with the compounding period.

PROGRAM LISTING

PRESENT VALUE ANALYSIS

```
100 CALL CLEAR
110 PRINT "WHAT IS THE"
120 PRINT "FUTURE VALUE";
130 INPUT FV
140 PRINT
150 PRINT "WHAT IS THE ANNUAL"
160 PRINT "INTEREST RATE";
170 INPUT I
180 I=I/100
190 CALL CLEAR
200 PRINT "WHAT IS THE"
210 PRINT "COMPOUNDING PERIOD?"
220 PRINT
230 PRINT
240 PRINT "ENTER"
250 PRINT
260 PRINT
270 PRINT TAB(5);"365 FOR DAILY"
280 PRINT TAB(5);"52 FOR WEEKLY"
290 PRINT TAB(5);"12 FOR MONTHLY"
300 PRINT TAB(5);"4 FOR QUARTERLY"
310 PRINT TAB(5);"2 FOR SEMI-ANNUALLY"
320 PRINT TAB(5);"1 FOR ANNUALLY"
330 PRINT
340 PRINT
350 INPUT CP
360 CALL CLEAR
370 PRINT "HOW MANY YEARS FROM"
```

Note: If using the TI Professional Computer, substitute PRINT CHR$(12) for CALL CLEAR.

```
380 PRINT "NOW IS THE"
390 PRINT "FUTURE VALUE";
400 INPUT P
410 N = INT(P*CP)
420 K = I/CP
430 PV = FV/(1+K)^N
440 PV = INT((PV+.005)*100)/100
450 CALL CLEAR
460 PRINT "PRESENT VALUE ="
470 PRINT "$";PV
480 END
```

Present Value of an Annuity Analysis
16

In this section we'll learn how to use the TI-99/4A to determine the present value of an annuity. As you may remember from our earlier discussion, an annuity is a regular series of payments. The payments need not occur on an annual basis. They can be made at the end of a week, month, quarter, or any other regular time interval.

Several applications will be reviewed in this chapter. We'll learn how to take payments to be received in the future back to their present value. We'll also see the effects of varying the interest rate and compounding period.

SAMPLE ANALYSIS: EXACT ACCOUNT DEPLETION

Kathy Brown is going to purchase a new boat. She is taking out a 48-month loan with payments of $222.56. Ms. Brown could pay cash for the boat if she wanted to, but she has chosen instead to set up a special bank account. Ms. Brown wants to put just enough money in the account so that when the last payment is made, the account will be depleted. The bank pays 14 percent interest, compounded daily. How much money should Ms. Brown deposit in the account?

Solving this problem requires finding the present value of a 48-month annuity, with payments of $222.56, 14 percent interest, and daily compounding. We can use the Present Value of an Annuity program to do this. Load the program beginning on page 152 into your TI-99/4A, enter the command RUN, and here's what the computer will ask for:

Computer Request	Operator Input
WHAT IS THE PERIODIC PAYMENT?	222.56
HOW OFTEN IS IT MADE? ENTER	
365 FOR DAILY	
52 FOR WEEKLY	
12 FOR MONTHLY	
4 FOR QUARTERLY	
2 FOR SEMI-ANNUALLY	
1 FOR ANNUALLY	
?	12
WHAT IS THE INTEREST RATE?	14
WHAT IS THE INTEREST COMPOUNDING PERIOD? ENTER	
365 FOR DAILY	
52 FOR WEEKLY	
12 FOR MONTHLY	
4 FOR QUARTERLY	
2 FOR SEMI-ANNUALLY	
1 FOR ANNUALLY	
?	365
FOR HOW MANY YEARS WILL PAYMENTS BE MADE?	4

At this point, the screen will clear and the computer will provide the answer:

PRESENT VALUE = $8132.64

** DONE **

This means Ms. Brown will have to deposit $8132.64 in the bank. If she does that, she can make 48 payments of $222.56, and have no money left in the account after the final payment.

SAMPLE ANALYSIS: COMPARING PAYMENT METHODS

Hillman Industries builds truck cabs. Hillman has two truck companies interested in buying all the cabs Hillman can produce in the next year. The first company has offered to pay for all of the cabs right away, at a total cost of $150,000. The second company has offered to pay $14,000 each month. If the effective annual interest rate is 13 percent, which offer should Hillman accept?

Solving this problem requires determining the present value of the $14,000 monthly annuity and seeing whether it exceeds the $150,000 lump sum the first company is willing to pay. Hillman should select whichever is greater, because the greater amount represents the largest profit. Let's run the Present Value of an Annuity program to find out what the annuity is worth today:

Computer Request	Operator Input
WHAT IS THE PERIODIC PAYMENT?	14000
HOW OFTEN IS IT MADE?	
ENTER	
365 FOR DAILY	
52 FOR WEEKLY	
12 FOR MONTHLY	
4 FOR QUARTERLY	
2 FOR SEMI-ANNUALLY	
1 FOR ANNUALLY	
?	12
WHAT IS THE INTEREST RATE?	13
WHAT IS THE INTEREST COMPOUNDING PERIOD?	
ENTER	
365 FOR DAILY	
12 FOR MONTHLY	
4 FOR QUARTERLY	
2 FOR SEMI-ANNUALLY	
1 FOR ANNUALLY	
?	1
FOR HOW MANY YEARS WILL PAYMENTS BE MADE?	1

Once you've entered the above data, the screen will clear, and the computer will provide the answer:

PRESENT VALUE = $148672.57

** DONE **

Since the present value of the annuity is less than the $150,000 lump sum the other company is offering, Hillman should opt for the lump sum payment.

SAMPLE ANALYSIS: ADJUSTING FOR INTEREST-RATE CHANGES

Suppose the interest rate in the problem above dropped to 10 percent. What should Hillman do in that case?

We can solve this problem in exactly the same manner as we did above, changing the interest rate to 10 percent:

Computer Request	Operator Input
WHAT IS THE PERIODIC PAYMENT?	14000
HOW OFTEN IS IT MADE?	
ENTER	
365 FOR DAILY	
52 FOR WEEKLY	
12 FOR MONTHLY	
4 FOR QUARTERLY	
2 FOR SEMI-ANNUALLY	
1 FOR ANNUALLY	
?	12
WHAT IS THE INTEREST RATE?	10
WHAT IS THE INTEREST COMPOUNDING PERIOD?	
ENTER	
365 FOR DAILY	
52 FOR WEEKLY	
12 FOR MONTHLY	
4 FOR QUARTERLY	

Computer Request	Operator Input
2 FOR SEMI-ANNUALLY	
1 FOR ANNUALLY	
?	1
FOR HOW MANY YEARS WILL PAYMENTS BE MADE?	1

Once you've entered the above information, the screen will clear, and the computer will provide the answer:

PRESENT VALUE = $152727.27

** DONE **

In this case, Hillman should select the company offering the $14,000 monthly payments, since the present value of the monthly payments is higher.

Seeing a higher dollar amount associated with a lower interest rate may be confusing. In the second example, a 13-percent annuity yielded a present value of $148,672.57. When we dropped the interest rate to 10 percent, the present value of the annuity *increased* to $152,727.27. The reason for this is that we are dealing with present values, and if we lower the interest rate, we'll need to start out with a larger present value to meet the annuity payments.

SAMPLE ANALYSIS: ADJUSTING THE COMPOUNDING RATES

In this example we're going to throw a new wrinkle into the Hillman problem. Suppose the interest rate is still 13 percent, but now daily compounding will be used. In this case, which deal should Hillman accept?

Let's turn to the TI-99/4A again, and see what the best deal is. We'll run the problem exactly as we did in the last example, but we'll use daily instead of annual compounding:

Computer Request	Operator Input
WHAT IS THE PERIODIC PAYMENT	14000
HOW OFTEN IS IT MADE?	
ENTER	
365 FOR DAILY	
52 FOR WEEKLY	
12 FOR MONTHLY	

Computer Request	Operator Input
4 FOR QUARTERLY 2 FOR SEMI-ANNUALLY 1 FOR ANNUALLY	
?	12
WHAT IS THE INTEREST RATE?	13

WHAT IS THE INTEREST
COMPOUNDING PERIOD?
ENTER
   365 FOR DAILY
   52 FOR WEEKLY
   12 FOR MONTHLY
   4 FOR QUARTERLY
   2 FOR SEMI-ANNUALLY
   1 FOR ANNUALLY	

?	365
FOR HOW MANY YEARS WILL PAYMENTS BE MADE?	1

At this point, the screen will clear, and the computer will provide the answer:

PRESENT VALUE = $156688.35

** DONE **

In this case, the monthly payments have a larger present value than the $150,000 lump sum payment. Hillman should select the annuity payment schedule when daily compounding is used. Understanding why this is so requires a little insight. When we used annual compounding in the second example, none of the monthly payments had a chance to earn any interest, since they were all deposited before the first compounding period (which was one year). With daily compounding, though, each payment starts accruing interest as soon as it is made because the compounding period is less than the payment period. For that reason, the annuity has a higher present value with daily compounding than with annual compounding.

FORMULAS

Formulas are included in the Program Listing; they are reviewed here for ease of reference.

PRESENT VALUE OF AN ANNUITY

If the periodic payment occurs at the same time as, or more often than, the compounding period:

$$PV = PP \sum_{i=1}^{N} 1/(1 + I/CP)^{J_i} \quad \text{(see program lines 540 and 590-610)}$$

If the periodic payment occurs less frequently than the compounding period:

$$PV = PP \sum_{i=1}^{P*T} 1/(1 + I/CP)^{J_i*CP/T} \text{(see program lines 540 and 630-650)}$$

where

PV = present value of an annuity
PP = periodic payment
I = nominal, or stated, annual interest rate
CP = compounding period
N = number of compounding periods
J_i = number of the compounding period
T = number of payments per year
P = number of years

The implicit assumption in the above formulas is that the frequency of calculating and crediting interest coincides with the compounding period.

PROGRAM LISTING

PRESENT VALUE OF AN ANNUITY ANALYSIS

```
100 CALL CLEAR
110 PRINT "WHAT IS THE"
120 PRINT "PERIODIC PAYMENT";
130 INPUT PP
140 PRINT
150 PRINT "HOW OFTEN IS IT MADE?"
160 PRINT
```

Note: If using the TI Professional Computer, substitute PRINT CHR$(12) for CALL CLEAR.

```
170 PRINT
180 PRINT "ENTER"
190 PRINT
200 PRINT
210 PRINT TAB(5);"365 FOR DAILY"
220 PRINT TAB(5);"52 FOR WEEKLY"
230 PRINT TAB(5);"12 FOR MONTHLY"
240 PRINT TAB(5);"4 FOR QUARTERLY"
250 PRINT TAB(5);"2 FOR SEMI-ANNUALLY"
260 PRINT TAB(5);"1 FOR ANNUALLY"
270 PRINT
280 INPUT T
290 CALL CLEAR
300 PRINT "WHAT IS THE"
310 PRINT "INTEREST RATE";
320 INPUT I
330 I = I/100
340 PRINT
350 PRINT "WHAT IS THE INTEREST"
360 PRINT "COMPOUNDING PERIOD?"
370 PRINT
380 PRINT
390 PRINT "ENTER"
400 PRINT
410 PRINT
420 PRINT TAB(5);"365 FOR DAILY"
430 PRINT TAB(5);"52 FOR WEEKLY"
440 PRINT TAB(5);"12 FOR MONTHLY"
450 PRINT TAB(5);"4 FOR QUARTERLY"
460 PRINT TAB(5);"2 FOR SEMI-ANNUALLY"
470 PRINT TAB(5);"1 FOR ANNUALLY"
480 PRINT
490 INPUT CP
500 PRINT
510 PRINT "FOR HOW MANY YEARS WILL"
520 PRINT "PAYMENTS BE MADE";
530 INPUT P
540 K = I/CP
550 N = INT(CP*P)
560 PV = 0
570 IF T<CP THEN 630
580 PP = PP*(T/CP)
590 FOR J = 1 TO N
600 PV = PV + PP/(1+K)∧J
610 NEXT J
620 GO TO 660
```

```
630 FOR J=1 TO P*T
640 PV=PV+PP/(1+K)^((CP/T)*J)
650 NEXT J
660 PV=INT((PV+.005)*100)/100
670 CALL CLEAR
680 PRINT "PRESENT VALUE = $";PV
690 END
```

Perpetuity Analysis
17

In the previous chapters we covered the concepts of present and future values. We examined the effects of interest rate and compounding periods, and we reviewed some of the investment decisions these analyses can be used for.

One concept we haven't examined yet is that of a perpetuity. A perpetuity is simply a fund that pays an annuity forever (or *in perpetuity,* hence the name). If we can find the present value of a perpetuity, we'll know how much money to deposit if we wish to receive a never-ending series of regular payments. The concept can also be used to make some investment decisions.

We'll consider two types: an immediate perpetuity and a deferred perpetuity. As the names imply, the payments of an immediate perpetuity begin right away, while the payments of a deferred perpetuity will begin at a later date.

SAMPLE ANALYSIS: AN IMMEDIATE PERPETUITY

Frank Noble wants to set up a fund that will pay his daughter $500 a year for the rest of her life. If Frank's bank pays 12 percent interest, compounded annually, how much should he deposit in the fund?

Since Frank has no way of knowing how many years the fund will have to make the payment, he knows he should establish a perpetuity. In effect, he wants to know the present value of a perpetuity that pays 500 dollars annually. We can use the Perpetuity Analysis program to do this. Load the program into your TI-99/4A (the listing begins on page 160), enter the command RUN, and here's what the computer will ask for:

Computer Request	Operator Input
ENTER 1 FOR AN IMMEDIATE PERPETUITY	
ENTER 2 FOR A DEFERRED PERPETUITY	
?	1
WHAT IS THE PERPETUITY PAYMENT AMOUNT?	500
HOW OFTEN IS IT MADE? ENTER	
365 FOR DAILY	
52 FOR WEEKLY	
12 FOR MONTHLY	
4 FOR QUARTERLY	
2 FOR SEMI-ANNUALLY	
1 FOR ANNUALLY	
?	1
WHAT IS THE INTEREST COMPOUNDING PERIOD? ENTER	
365 FOR DAILY	
52 FOR WEEKLY	
12 FOR MONTHLY	
4 FOR QUARTERLY	
2 FOR SEMI-ANNUALLY	
1 FOR ANNUALLY	
?	1
WHAT IS THE INTEREST RATE?	12

At this point, the screen will clear and the computer will provide the answer:

THE PRESENT VALUE OF THE
PERPETUITY IS $4166.77

** DONE **

SAMPLE ANALYSIS: A DEFERRED PERPETUITY

Wil Maxton wants to set up a fund that will pay him $1200 per month when he retires in 25 years. If Mr. Maxton's bank pays 11 percent interest (compounded monthly), how much should Wil deposit in the bank today?

This problem is similar to the one above, except now we are working with a deferred perpetuity. Let's run the Perpetuity Analysis program again, and see how much Mr. Maxton should deposit.

Computer Request	Operator Input
ENTER 1 FOR AN IMMEDIATE PERPETUITY	
ENTER 2 FOR A DEFERRED PERPETUITY	
?	2
WHAT IS THE PERPETUITY PAYMENT AMOUNT?	1200
HOW OFTEN IS IT MADE?	
ENTER	
365 FOR DAILY	
52 FOR WEEKLY	
12 FOR MONTHLY	
4 FOR QUARTERLY	
2 FOR SEMI-ANNUALLY	
1 FOR ANNUALLY	
?	12
WHAT IS THE INTEREST COMPOUNDING PERIOD?	
ENTER	
365 FOR DAILY	
52 FOR WEEKLY	
12 FOR MONTHLY	
4 FOR QUARTERLY	
2 FOR SEMI-ANNUALLY	
1 FOR ANNUALLY	
?	12
WHAT IS THE INTEREST RATE?	11
FOR HOW MANY YEARS IS THE PERPETUITY PAYMENT TO BE DEFERRED?	25

Once you've entered the above data, the computer will provide the answer:

```
THE PRESENT VALUE OF THE
DEFERRED PERPETUITY
IS $8474.24
** DONE **
```

In other words, if Mr. Maxton deposits $8,474.24 in the bank today (and leaves the money in the bank), the account will make a monthly payment of $1,200 when he retires. The payments will go on as long as Mr. Maxton lives. Actually, since the account is a perpetuity, the payments would go on to his heirs.

SAMPLE ANALYSIS: PERPETUITY VS. CASH SETTLEMENT

Cliff Conover runs a dairy farm. The power company wants to build a substation on 20 acres Mr. Conover owns, and he has agreed to sell the land. The power company has offered to pay Mr. Conover either $500,000 (after taxes) as an outright cash settlement, or $20,000 per year (after taxes) for life. If Mr. Conover's bank pays 9 percent interest (compounded daily), which is the better offer?

Finding the answer to this problem requires only that we determine the present value of the $20,000 dollar perpetuity. If it exceeds $500,000, the perpetuity should be selected. If the $500,000 cash settlement is greater than the present value of the perpetuity, the cash settlement is preferable. Let's run the Perpetuity Analysis program to see what Mr. Conover should do.

Computer Request	Operator Input
ENTER 1 FOR AN IMMEDIATE PERPETUITY	
ENTER 2 FOR A DEFERRED PERPETUITY	
?	1
WHAT IS THE PERPETUITY PAYMENT AMOUNT?	20000
HOW OFTEN IS IT MADE? ENTER 365 FOR DAILY 52 FOR WEEKLY	

Computer Request	Operator Input
12 FOR MONTHLY 4 FOR QUARTERLY 2 FOR SEMI-ANNUALLY 1 FOR ANNUALLY	
?	1
WHAT IS THE INTEREST COMPOUNDING PERIOD? ENTER 365 FOR DAILY 52 FOR WEEKLY 12 FOR MONTHLY 4 FOR QUARTERLY 2 FOR SEMI-ANNUALLY 1 FOR ANNUALLY	
?	365
WHAT IS THE INTEREST RATE?	9

At this point, the screen will clear, and the computer will provide the answer:

THE PRESENT VALUE OF THE
PERPETUITY IS $212399.58

** DONE **

Since the present value of the perpetuity is less than the $500,000 the power company is offering as a cash price, Mr. Conover should accept the $500,000. He could put $212,399.58 of that money in the bank (which is the present value of a $20,000 annual perpetuity) and still get the $20,000 annual payment for life. Then he'd have almost $300,000 left over for other purposes.

FORMULAS

Formulas are included in the Program Listing, and reviewed here for ease of reference.

PRESENT VALUE OF A PERPETUITY

If the periodic payment occurs at the same time as, or less frequently than, the compounding period:

$$V = P/[(1 + I/CP)^{CP/T} - 1] \quad \text{(see program line 600)}$$

If the periodic payment occurs more often than the compounding period:

$$V = P*T/CP + T*P/I \quad \text{(see program line 620)}$$

where

V = present value of the perpetuity
P = perpetuity payment amount
I = nominal, or stated, annual interest rate
CP = compounding period
T = number of payments per year

PRESENT VALUE OF A DEFERRED PERPETUITY

$$PV = V/(1 + I/CP)^N \quad \text{(see program lines 740-760)}$$

where

PV = present value of a deferred perpetuity
V = value of deferred perpetuity at end of deferral period (i.e., when the payments begin)
I = nominal, or stated, annual interest rate
CP = compounding period
N = number of compounding periods during deferral period

The implicit assumption in these formulas is that the frequency of calculating and crediting interest coincides with the compounding period.

PROGRAM LISTING

PERPETUITY ANALYSIS

```
100 CALL CLEAR
110 PRINT "ENTER 1 FOR AN"
120 PRINT "IMMEDIATE PERPETUITY"
130 PRINT
140 PRINT "ENTER 2 FOR A"
150 PRINT "DEFERRED PERPETUITY"
160 PRINT
170 INPUT PP
180 PRINT
190 PRINT "WHAT IS THE"
200 PRINT "PERPETUITY PAYMENT"
```

Note: If using the TI Professional Computer, substitute PRINT CHR$(12) for CALL CLEAR.

```
210 PRINT "AMOUNT";
220 INPUT P
230 CALL CLEAR
240 PRINT "HOW OFTEN IS IT MADE?"
250 PRINT
260 PRINT
270 PRINT "ENTER"
280 PRINT
290 PRINT
300 PRINT TAB(5);"365 FOR DAILY"
310 PRINT TAB(5);"52 FOR WEEKLY"
320 PRINT TAB(5);"12 FOR MONTHLY"
330 PRINT TAB(5);"4 FOR QUARTERLY"
340 PRINT TAB(5);"2 FOR SEMI-ANNUALLY"
350 PRINT TAB(5);"1 FOR ANNUALLY"
360 PRINT
370 INPUT T
380 CALL CLEAR
390 PRINT "WHAT IS THE INTEREST"
400 PRINT "COMPOUNDING PERIOD?"
410 PRINT
420 PRINT
430 PRINT "ENTER"
440 PRINT
450 PRINT
460 PRINT TAB(5);"365 FOR DAILY"
470 PRINT TAB(5);"52 FOR WEEKLY"
480 PRINT TAB(5);"12 FOR MONTHLY"
490 PRINT TAB(5);"4 FOR QUARTERLY"
500 PRINT TAB(5);"2 FOR SEMI-ANNUALLY"
510 PRINT TAB(5);"1 FOR ANNUALLY"
520 PRINT
530 INPUT CP
540 CALL CLEAR
550 PRINT "WHAT IS THE"
560 PRINT "INTEREST RATE";
570 INPUT I
580 I=I/100
590 IF CP< T THEN 620
600 V=P/((1+I/CP)^(CP/T)-1)
610 GO TO 630
620 V=P*T/CP+T*P/I
630 V=INT((V+.005)*100)/100
640 IF PP=2 THEN 690
650 CALL CLEAR
660 PRINT "THE PRESENT VALUE OF THE"
670 PRINT "PERPETUITY IS $";V
```

```
680 GO TO 820
690 PRINT
700 PRINT "FOR HOW MANY YEARS"
710 PRINT "IS THE PERPETUITY PAYMENT TO"
720 PRINT "BE DEFERRED";
730 INPUT N
740 N=INT(N*CP)
750 K=I/CP
760 V=V/(1+K)^N
770 V=INT((V+.005)*100)/100
780 CALL CLEAR
790 PRINT "THE PRESENT VALUE OF THE"
800 PRINT "DEFERRED PERPETUITY"
810 PRINT "IS $";V
820 END
```

Net Present Value Analysis
18

In the Chapters 16 and 17 we discussed the concepts of present value for both fixed amounts and annuities. In the examples we examined, we wanted to find the present value of money that would be received in the future. We were interested in knowing how much to invest today (or over a period of time) to reach a specified amount, or in finding the investment that required the lowest initial cash outlay.

The corporate financial analyst usually takes an approach that may appear to do just the opposite. Corporate investments are usually based on the concept that the fundamental objective of any business is to maximize its wealth. To accomplish this objective, a comparison of the present value of investment alternatives is often used.

This comparison is generally referred to as net present value analysis. *Net present value analysis* simply assesses the present values of available investments (subtracting the present value of alternative project costs from the present value of the anticipated returns). The project with the highest net present value represents the investment choice that maximizes the wealth of the company. This investment option is the one the company should select.

SAMPLE ANALYSIS: THREE OIL-EXPLORATION PROJECTS

Orion Industries is engaged in the offshore oil exploration business. The company is in the process of deciding whether to drill in the North Sea, the Gulf of Mexico, or off the southern coast of California.

If Orion drills for oil in the North Sea, a new drilling vessel that can operate in rough seas will be necessary. The new ship will cost one million dollars. The company expects to earn two million dollars each year for four years from the North Sea project.

Orion can use one of its existing ships to start drilling off the coast of southern California, but the ship will have to be refurbished at a cost of $10,000. The company expects to realize the following returns at the end of each year for the southern California project:

Year	Return
1	$500,000
2	1,500,000
3	2,000,000

After the end of the third year, no other returns are expected from the California drilling operation.

Orion can use the same ship for the Gulf of Mexico venture, but in addition to the $10,000 for refurbishment, additional sailing costs will be incurred in the amount of $15,000. The Gulf of Mexico project is expected to return $750,000 at the end of the first year, and one million dollars per year for the next three years. No returns are expected after the end of the fourth year.

Orion's cost of capital is 14 percent, which is an effective annual interest rate.

We can use the Net Present Value Analysis program to determine the investment that provides the greatest present value to Orion Industries. To do this, let's load the program into the computer (the listing begins on page 168), enter the command RUN, and find the investment option that maximizes the wealth of Orion Industries:

Computer Request	Operator Input
HOW MANY PROJECTS ARE TO BE EXAMINED?	3
WHAT IS THE NAME OF PROJECT 1?	NORTH SEA
WHAT IS THE LIFE OF NORTH SEA?	4

Computer Request	Operator Input
HOW MANY START-UP COSTS ARE ASSOCIATED WITH NORTH SEA?	1
WHAT IS THE NAME OF PROJECT 2?	SOUTHERN CALIFORNIA
WHAT IS THE LIFE OF SOUTHERN CALIFORNIA?	3
HOW MANY START-UP COSTS ARE ASSOCIATED WITH SOUTHERN CALIFORNIA?	1
WHAT IS THE NAME OF PROJECT 3?	GULF OF MEXICO
WHAT IS THE LIFE OF GULF OF MEXICO?	4
HOW MANY START-UP COSTS ARE ASSOCIATED WITH GULF OF MEXICO?	2
WHAT IS THE INTEREST RATE?	14

WHAT IS THE
COMPOUNDING PERIOD?

ENTER

    365 FOR DAILY
    52 FOR WEEKLY
    12 FOR MONTHLY
    4 FOR QUARTERLY
    2 FOR SEMI-ANNUALLY
    1 FOR ANNUALLY

?   1

WILL THE RETURNS FROM
THE NORTH SEA PROJECT BE
AN ANNUITY OR
AN UNEVEN SERIES?

ENTER

    1 FOR AN ANNUITY
    2 FOR AN UNEVEN SERIES

?   1

| WHAT IS THE ANNUAL RETURN? | 2000000 |

Computer Request	Operator Input
WHAT IS START-UP COST 1 FOR THE NORTH SEA PROJECT?	1000000

WILL THE RETURNS FROM
THE SOUTHERN CALIFORNIA
PROJECT BE
AN ANNUITY OR
AN UNEVEN SERIES?

ENTER

    1 FOR AN ANNUITY
    2 FOR AN UNEVEN SERIES

?	2
WHAT IS THE RETURN FOR YEAR 1?	500000
WHAT IS THE RETURN FOR YEAR 2?	1500000
WHAT IS THE RETURN FOR YEAR 3?	2000000
WHAT IS START-UP COST 1 FOR THE SOUTHERN CALIFORNIA PROJECT?	10000

WILL THE RETURNS FROM
THE GULF OF MEXICO
PROJECT BE
AN ANNUITY OR
AN UNEVEN SERIES?

ENTER

    1 FOR AN ANNUITY
    2 FOR AN UNEVEN SERIES

?	2
WHAT IS THE RETURN FOR YEAR 1?	750000
WHAT IS THE RETURN FOR YEAR 2?	1000000
WHAT IS THE RETURN FOR YEAR 3?	1000000
WHAT IS THE RETURN FOR YEAR 4?	1000000

Computer Request	Operator Input
WHAT IS START-UP COST 1 FOR THE GULF OF MEXICO PROJECT?	10000
WHAT IS START-UP COST 2 FOR THE GULF OF MEXICO PROJECT?	15000

At this point, the screen will clear, and the computer will provide the answer:

NET PRESENT VALUE OF THE
NORTH SEA PROJECT IS
$ 4827424.61

NET PRESENT VALUE OF THE
SOUTHERN CALIFORNIA
PROJECT IS
$ 2932740.82

NET PRESENT VALUE OF THE
GULF OF MEXICO PROJECT IS
$ 2669414.06

** DONE **

Orion should select the North Sea project, since it has the greatest net present value. Even though the North Sea project requires the greatest initial cash outlay, it has the potential for the largest increase in the wealth of the company.

FORMULAS

Formulas are included in the Program Listing; they are reviewed here for ease of reference.

PRESENT VALUE OF ANNUAL RETURNS

$$PV \sum_{i=1}^{N} R_i/(1 + I/CP)^{i*CP} \quad \text{(see program lines 740-790 and 810-870)}$$

where

PV = present value of annual returns
R_i = return for the ith year
I = nominal, or stated, annual interest rate

CP = compounding period
J_i = number of the compounding period
N = number of years

NET PRESENT VALUE

$$NPV = PV - TOTCOST \quad \text{(see program line 960)}$$

where

NPV = net present value
PV = present value of annual returns
$TOTCOST$ = total start-up costs

The implicit assumption in these formulas is that the frequency of calculating and crediting interest coincides with the compounding period.

PROGRAM LISTING

NET PRESENT VALUE ANALYSIS

```
100 CALL CLEAR
110 DIM PP$(25),N(25),SC(25),NPV(25),COST(25)
120 PRINT "HOW MANY PROJECTS"
130 PRINT "ARE TO BE EXAMINED";
140 INPUT P
150 FOR Q=1 TO P
160 PRINT
170 PRINT "WHAT IS THE NAME"
180 PRINT "OF PROJECT ";Q;
190 INPUT PP$(Q)
200 PRINT
210 PRINT "WHAT IS THE LIFE"
220 PRINT "OF ";PP$(Q);
230 INPUT N(Q)
240 PRINT
250 PRINT "HOW MANY START-UP"
260 PRINT "COSTS ARE ASSOCIATED"
270 PRINT "WITH ";PP$(Q);
280 INPUT SC(Q)
290 NEXT Q
300 CALL CLEAR
310 PRINT "WHAT IS THE"
```

Note: If using the TI Professional Computer, substitute PRINT CHR$(12) for CALL CLEAR.

```
320 PRINT "INTEREST RATE";
330 INPUT I
340 I = I/100
350 PRINT
360 PRINT "WHAT IS THE"
370 PRINT "COMPOUNDING PERIOD?"
380 PRINT
390 PRINT
400 PRINT "ENTER"
410 PRINT
420 PRINT
430 PRINT TAB(5);"365 FOR DAILY"
440 PRINT TAB(5);"52 FOR WEEKLY"
450 PRINT TAB(5);"12 FOR MONTHLY"
460 PRINT TAB(5);"4 FOR QUARTERLY"
470 PRINT TAB(5);"2 FOR SEMI-ANNUALLY"
480 PRINT TAB(5);"1 FOR ANNUALLY"
490 PRINT
500 INPUT CP
510 K = I/CP
520 CALL CLEAR
530 FOR Q = 1 TO P
540 PV = 0
550 TOTCOST = 0
560 CALL CLEAR
570 PRINT "WILL THE RETURNS FROM"
580 PRINT "THE ";PP$(Q);" PROJECT BE"
590 PRINT "AN ANNUITY OR"
600 PRINT "AN UNEVEN SERIES?"
610 PRINT
620 PRINT
630 PRINT "ENTER"
640 PRINT
650 PRINT
660 PRINT TAB(5);"1 FOR AN ANNUITY"
670 PRINT TAB(5);"2 FOR AN UNEVEN SERIES"
680 PRINT
690 INPUT AN
700 IF AN = 2 THEN 810
710 IF AN = 1 THEN 730
720 GO TO 560
730 PRINT
740 PRINT "WHAT IS THE ANNUAL"
750 PRINT "RETURN";
760 INPUT R
770 FOR J = 1 TO N(Q)
780 PV = PV + R/(1 + K)^(J*CP)
```

```
790 NEXT J
800 GO TO 880
810 FOR J=1 TO N(Q)
820 PRINT
830 PRINT "WHAT IS THE RETURN"
840 PRINT "FOR YEAR ";J;
850 INPUT R
860 PV=PV+R/(1+K)∧(J*CP)
870 NEXT J
880 FOR J=1 TO SC(Q)
890 PRINT
900 PRINT "WHAT IS START-UP COST ";J
910 PRINT "FOR THE "; PP$(Q)
920 PRINT "PROJECT";
930 INPUT COST(J)
940 TOTCOST=TOTCOST+COST(J)
950 NEXT J
960 NPV(Q)=PV−TOTCOST
970 NPV(Q)=INT((NPV(Q)+.005)*100)/100
980 NEXT Q
990 CALL CLEAR
1000 FOR Q=1 TO P
1010 PRINT "NET PRESENT VALUE OF THE"
1020 PRINT PP$(Q);" PROJECT IS"
1030 PRINT "$"; NPV(Q)
1040 PRINT
1050 PRINT
1060 NEXT Q
1070 END
```

Index

accelerated depreciation, 51-52
account depletion, exact, 146-147
accounts receivable, collection of, 1
additional funds needed (to support sales increase), formula, 32
administrative expenses, 21
annual carrying cost of safety stock, formula, 98
annual returns, present value formula, 167-168
annualized cost of not taking discount, formula, 115
annuity, 130
   calculation of varied amounts, 133-135
   future value analysis of, 130-138
   future value formula, 136
   present value of, 146-154
   present value formula, 152
asset cost, and depreciation, 50
asset management, 7
asset management ratios, 1
average collection period, 1, 7
   formula, 8
average delivery time, formula, 96
average demand rate, formula, 96-97
average inventory, formula, 96

balance sheet, and pro forma forecasting analysis, 25
beta, 102
beta coefficients, 102-103
beta of portfolio, 103-104
   formula, 111
borrowing. *See* Debt
bottom line, corporate, 2
brokerage commissions, 108

capital
   analysis of cost, 35-49
   appreciation, 102
   formula for weighted average cost of, 44-45
capital structure
   current, 36, 38
   resulting, 36-37
carrying costs, of inventory, 90, 91
   formula for total annual, 97-98
cash settlement, compared to perpetuity, 158-159
coefficient of correlation. *See* Correlation coefficient
collection period, average, 1, 7
   formula, 8

common stock
　formula for cost, 44
　as part of capital structure, 36
compounding interest, 117
　continuous, 120, 122
　daily, 119, 120
　effect on future value, 126
　and present value of annuity analysis, 150-151
confidence interval, 64, 69, 93
　formula, 78, 86
confidence limits, 64, 69-70
continuous compounding, 120, 122
corporate investments, 163
　example, 164-167
corporate performance assessment, 2-7
correlation analysis, 62-80
　limitations of, 73
correlation coefficient, 62-63
　formula, 77
cost of capital, 35-49
　current, 36
　and debt, 35
　formula for weighted average, 44-45
　marginal, 36, 43
cost of common stock, formula, 44
cost of debt, formula, 44
cost of goods sold, 18
cost of not taking discount, 114
　formula, 115
cost of preferred stock, formula, 44
cost-volume-profit analysis, 21
costs. *See also* Fixed costs; Variable costs for sales increases, 26-31
current assets ratio, 1
　formula, 7-8
current capital structure, 36
current cost of capital, 36

debt
　and cost of capital, 35
　formula for cost, 44
　as part of capital structure, 36
debt management ratios, 2
debt ratio, 2, 7
　ceilings on, 37, 43
　formula, 9
declining balance depreciation, 52
　formula, 58
deferred perpetuity, 155, 157-158
　present value formula, 160
delivery schedule, 92
　and safety stock, 91

delivery time
　formula for average, 96
　formula for standard deviation, 96
demand rate
　formula for average, 96-97
　formula for standard deviation, 97
　and safety stock, 91
dependent variables, 64
　and correlation coefficient, 62
　and multiple linear regression analysis, 81
　value prediction with regression analysis, 63-64
depletion, exact, of account, 146-147
depreciation analysis, 50-61
discount, formula for cost of not taking, 115
discount analysis, 114-116

economic ordering quantity, 90, 91, 93
　formula, 95-96
effective annual interest rate
　analysis, 117-124
　formula, 122-123
　relation to present value analysis, 143
equipment
　and fixed assets ratio, 1
　and sales increases, 26
exact account depletion, 146-147
expected market rate of return, 102
expected rate of return, 102, 110
expected return of portfolio
　formula, 111
　relation with beta, 104

financial ratio analysis, 1-14
financing, cost as marginal cost of capital, 36
fixed assets ratio, 1, 7
　formula, 8-9
fixed costs, 21
　of inventory, 91
fixed return, and present value analysis, 139-140
forecasting analysis, pro forma financial, 25-34
formulas
　additional funds needed, 32
　annual carrying cost of safety stock, 98
　annualized cost of not taking discount, 115
　average collection periods, 8
　average delivery time, 96
　average demand rate, 96-97
　average inventory, 96
　beta of portfolio, 111

INDEX

confidence interval, 78, 86
correlation coefficient, 77
cost of common stock, 44
cost of debt, 44
cost of preferred stock, 44
current assets ratio, 7-8
debt ratio, 9
declining balance depreciation, 58
economic ordering quantity, 95-96
effective annual interest rate, 122-123
expected return of portfolio, 111
fixed assets ratio, 8-9
future value, 128
future value of annuity, 136
inventory turnover ratio, 8
linear regression equation, 77
multiple linear regression equation, 85
net income, 23
net present value, 168
percent of sales, 19
portfolio value, 111
present value, 143-144
present value of annual returns, 167-168
present value of annuity, 152
present value of deferred perpetuity, 160
present value of perpetuity, 159-160
profit margin on sales ratio, 9
projected account increase, 31-32
quick ratio, 8
return on assets ratio, 10
return on equity ratio, 10
safety stock, 97
standard deviation, 77-78, 85-86
standard deviation of delivery time, 96
standard deviation of demand rate, 97
straight-line depreciation, 57
sum-of-the-years'-digits depreciation, 58
times interest earned ratio, 9
total annual carrying cost, 97-98
total assets ratio, 9
units of production depreciation, 57-58
weighted average cost of capital, 44
future value analysis, 125-129
    formula, 128
    relation to present value analysis, 143
future value of annuity, 130-138
    formula, 136

immediate perpetuity, 155-156
income statement, 15

independent variables, 64
    and correlation coefficient, 62
    and multiple linear regression analysis, 81
interest accrual, and compounding period, 151
interest payments, relation to earnings, 2
interest rate, effective annual
    formula, 122-123
    relation to present value analysis, 143
interest rate analysis, 117-124
interest rate compounding
    continuous, 120, 122
    daily, 119, 120
    effect on future value, 126
    and present value of annuity analysis, 150-151
interest rate adjustments
    and present value of annuity analysis, 149-150
inventory
    formula for average, 96
    and liquidity ratios, 1
inventory carrying costs, 90, 91
inventory level, optimal average, 90, 91, 93
inventory level analysis, 90-101
inventory turnover ratio, 1, 7
    formula, 8
investment, initial, 143

linear regression equation, formula, 77
liquidity ratios, 1

marginal cost of capital, 36, 43
market performance, and stock reaction, 103
market rate of return, 104
    expected, 102
multiple linear regression analysis, 81-90
    limitations, 81-82
multiple linear regression equation, formula, 85

negative betas, 103
negative correlation coefficient, 63
net income, 18
    forecasting, 21-22
    formula, 23
net present value, formula, 168
net present value analysis, 163-170
net profit margin, 2
new product development, 37-43
new projects, marginal cost of capital for, 36
normal depreciation, 50-51

optimal average inventory level, 90, 91, 93
ordering costs, 95
ordering quantity, optimal, 90
ordering quantity, optimal, 90
ordering quantity analysis. *See* Economic ordering quantity

payment methods comparison, and present value of annuity analysis, 148-149
percent income statement analysis, 15
percent of sales, formula, 19
performance assessment, corporate, 2-7
perpetuities, 155-162
    compared to cash settlement, 158-159
    present value formula, 159-160
plant facilities
    and fixed assets ratio, 1
    and sales increases, 26
portfolio
    analysis, 102-113
    defined, 102
    formula for expected return, 111
    formula for value, 111
positive correlation, 73, 76
positive correlation coefficient, 62
preferred stock
    formula for cost, 44
    as part of capital structure, 36
present value, 139-145
    analysis of net, 163-170
    determination of smallest, 140-143
    formula, 143-144
    formula for net, 168
present value of annual returns, formula, 167-168
present value of annuity, 146-154
    formula, 152
present value of perpetuity, 155
    formula, 159-160
    formula for deferred, 160
pro forma balance sheet, 25
pro forma financial forecasting analysis, 25-34
product mix, 22
profit margin on sales, 7
profit margin on sales ratio, 2
    formula, 9
profitability, trends restricting, 15-18
profitability ratios, 2, 7
projected account increase, formula, 31-32

property, and sales increases, 26
purchase price, of inventory, 91

quick assets ratio, 1
quick ratio, 7
    formula, 8

ROA. *See* Return on total assets
ROE. *See* Return on equity
rate of return, expected, 102, 110
rate of return, market, 104
    expected, 102
rate of return, risk-free, 102, 104
ratios, financial, 1-14
receiving costs, of inventory, 91
regression analysis, 62-80
    limitations of, 73
    limitations of multiple linear, 81-82
    multiple linear, 81-90
resulting capital structure, 36-37
retained earnings
    and cost of capital, 35
    as part of capital structure, 36
    on pro forma balance sheet, 26
return on assets, 7
    ratio formula, 10
return on equity, 2, 7
    ratio formula, 10
return expected from portfolio, formula, 111
return on total assets, 2
risk, 102, 104
    and beta value, 103
risk-free rate of return, 102, 104

safety stock, 90-93, 95
    annual carrying cost formula, 98
    formula, 97
sales
    and balance sheet entries, 25
    relation to income statement entries, 15
sales commissions, 18
sales increases, costs of, 26-31
salvage value, 50, 51
service life, of asset, 50
shipping costs, of inventory, 91
standard deviation, formula, 77-78, 85-86
standard deviation of delivery time, formula, 96
standard deviation of demand rate, formula, 97
stock dividends, 102

stock offerings, and cost of capital, 35
stockouts, 90, 91, 92, 95
stocks. *See also* Common stock; Preferred stock
    beta coefficients for, 103
straight-line depreciation, 50
    formula, 57
sum-of-the-years'-digits depreciation, 51
    formula, 58

taxes
    and accelerated depreciation, 51
    and depreciation, 50
time lag, in correlation analysis, 73
time value of money, 125
times interest earned ratio, 2, 7
    formula, 9

total annual carrying cost, formula, 97–98
total assets ratio, 1, 7
    formula, 9

U.S. Treasury securities, 102
units-of-production depreciation, 51
    formula, 57–58

variable costs, 21
    of inventory, 91
variable interest rate, 121
variables, 73. *See also* Dependent variables; Independent variables

weighted average cost of capital, formula, 44–45